C000253643

# SIGILS FOR SELF-CARE

## Psychological and Emotional
## Healing through Symbols

### D.R. T STEPHENS

**S.D.N Publishing**

Copyright © 2023 S.D.N Publishing

All rights reserved

The characters and events portrayed in this book are fictitious. Any similarity to real persons, living or dead, is coincidental and not intended by the author.

No part of this book may be reproduced, or stored in a retrieval system, or transmitted in any form or by any means, electronic, mechanical, photocopying, recording, or otherwise, without express written permission of the publisher.

ISBN: 9798863542942

# CONTENTS

# GENERAL DISCLAIMER

This book is intended to provide informative and educational material on the subject matter covered. The author(s), publisher, and any affiliated parties make no representations or warranties with respect to the accuracy, applicability, completeness, or suitability of the contents herein and specifically disclaim any implied warranties of merchantability or fitness for a particular purpose.

The information contained in this book is for general information purposes only and is not intended to serve as legal, medical, financial, or any other form of professional advice. Readers should consult with appropriate professionals before making any decisions based on the information provided. Neither the author(s) nor the publisher shall be held responsible or liable for any loss, damage, injury, claim, or otherwise, whether direct or indirect, consequential, or incidental, that may occur as a result of applying or misinterpreting the information in this book.

This book may contain references to third-party

websites, products, or services. Such references do not constitute an endorsement or recommendation, and the author(s) and publisher are not responsible for any outcomes related to these third-party references.

In no event shall the author(s), publisher, or any affiliated parties be liable for any direct, indirect, punitive, special, incidental, or other consequential damages arising directly or indirectly from any use of this material, which is provided "as is," and without warranties of any kind, express or implied.

By reading this book, you acknowledge and agree that you assume all risks and responsibilities concerning the applicability and consequences of the information provided. You also agree to indemnify, defend, and hold harmless the author(s), publisher, and any affiliated parties from any and all liabilities, claims, demands, actions, and causes of action whatsoever, whether or not foreseeable, that may arise from using or misusing the information contained in this book.

Although every effort has been made to ensure the accuracy of the information in this book as of the date of publication, the landscape of the subject matter covered is continuously evolving. Therefore, the author(s) and publisher expressly disclaim responsibility for any errors or omissions and reserve the right to update, alter, or revise the content without prior notice.

By continuing to read this book, you agree to be bound by the terms and conditions stated in this disclaimer. If you do not agree with these terms, it is your responsibility to discontinue use of this book immediately.

# CHAPTER 1: INTRODUCTION: THE ART AND SCIENCE OF SIGILS FOR SELF-CARE

Welcome to a transformative journey that bridges the mystical with the practical, the spiritual with the scientific, all for the sake of emotional and psychological well-being. If you've picked up this book, chances are you're seeking a new pathway to navigate through the complexities of your mental landscape. But why sigils? What can these intricate designs offer in the quest for a balanced and fulfilling life?

## Why Sigils Matter

Sigils are symbols, but they're not just any symbols. They're customized, highly personal designs that are imbued with your intention. Think of them as your own private language of empowerment, created by you, for you. In a world oversaturated with external messages, brands, and symbols, sigils offer a space for personal agency, carving out a mental and emotional realm where your intentions are front and center. You might be wondering if this idea of personal symbols is just another New Age fad, but rest assured, the concept has historical and cultural roots deeply entrenched in humanity's collective understanding of symbolism and its power to influence human behavior.

The art and science of sigil crafting span various disciplines. While the artistic aspect taps into your creativity and intuition, the scientific angle draws on psychological principles like priming, mental focus, and the theory of symbolic interactionism. This multidisciplinary approach allows for a richer, more nuanced understanding of how sigils can be effectively incorporated into self-care practices.

## Crafting Your Personal Lexicon

Creating your sigils is a two-fold process. The artistic phase involves free expression and imagination, serving as a meditative exercise that engages the right hemisphere of the brain, known for its role in creativity and emotional processing. The scientific part, meanwhile, leans on the left brain hemisphere, offering a structured framework for how to interpret and harness the power of these symbols. For example, we'll explore how the psychology of color affects perception and emotional response, offering guidelines on color choices for your sigils based on the psychological states you wish to induce or augment.

But what makes sigil crafting especially compelling is its highly individualized nature. Unlike generic symbols that have a predetermined meaning, the power of a sigil springs from your personal investment in its creation and interpretation. This ensures that the sigil resonates with your unique emotional and mental needs, rendering it a personalized tool in your arsenal for psychological resilience and emotional stability.

## Balancing Tradition and Modernity

Sigil crafting does not have to be an isolated practice disconnected from other therapeutic or self-care modalities. In fact, one of its strengths lies in its flexibility and adaptability. Traditional practices, like meditation or journaling, can be enhanced through the inclusion of personalized sigils. Similarly, the benefits of modern psychological approaches, such as Cognitive Behavioral Therapy, can be deepened through the integrative use of sigils that encapsulate therapeutic goals or affirmations.

The aim is not to replace other established therapeutic practices but to supplement them. Sigils can serve as a focal point during mindfulness exercises or act as a mnemonic device that triggers a particular emotional state. The complementary nature of sigil crafting makes it a valuable addition to any holistic approach to emotional and mental well-being.

So, whether you're a curious newcomer or a seasoned practitioner in various self-care modalities, this exploration into the world of sigils promises a creative, insightful, and profoundly personal experience. With each designed symbol, you're not just drawing; you're scribing your path to better emotional and psychological health. Welcome to the deeply empowering practice of crafting sigils for self-care.

# CHAPTER 2: THE HISTORICAL CONTEXT OF SIGILS AND SYMBOLISM

Welcome back! As you take your initial steps into the practice of crafting sigils for self-care, you might find yourself asking, "How did we get here?" Understanding the history and the symbolic landscape from which sigils evolved can offer a richer, more nuanced appreciation of this powerful tool. Today, we'll delve into the story of sigils and their symbolic cousins, looking at how they've found relevance across cultures, eras, and academic disciplines.

**From Cave Paintings to Modern Logos: A Brief Overview**

It's human nature to imbue meaning into visual representations. Take the prehistoric cave paintings for instance, like those found in the Chauvet Cave in France, dated back to around 30,000 years ago. These aren't just artistic impressions but carry within them the beliefs, hopes, and perhaps even rituals of ancient peoples. Some researchers suggest that they could have been a form of proto-writing or a way to communicate with the spiritual world. We've come a long way from the caves, but the essential process remains: using visual cues to encapsulate complex ideas or intentions.

Fast forward through history, and we see a vast tapestry of symbolism embedded in different cultural contexts. The Eye of Horus from ancient Egypt is an early example, often associated with protection, royal power, and good health. In medieval Europe, alchemists used an intricate array of symbols to represent substances and processes. Even today, think of how a simple 'swoosh' represents an entire ethos of athleticism and accomplishment, thanks to Nike's branding genius. Symbols speak a universal language, one that's richly layered and context-dependent but intrinsically linked to the human experience.

## Sigils in Religious and Magical Traditions

Sigils have a particularly strong history within religious and magical contexts. In Western esoteric traditions, they've been used in systems like Kabbalah and Hermeticism, often as intricate seals or signs designed to invoke angels, demons, or other spiritual entities. Sigils were tools of focused intention and were thought to draw or repel supernatural forces. They often incorporated complex geometrical shapes, planetary alignments, and sometimes even musical notations to harmonize with the frequency of the spiritual entity they aimed to invoke.

In Eastern traditions, similar practices exist, albeit with different names and symbolic languages. In Hinduism and Buddhism, for example, "yantras" and "mandalas" serve as focus points during meditation and are believed to have their own vibrational qualities. African traditions, such as the Adinkra symbols in Ghana, offer visual icons that encapsulate ethical principles, proverbs, and cultural narratives. Although the word "sigil" might be rooted in Western terminology, the practice and belief in the power of symbolic representation are remarkably universal.

## Sigils in Modern Psychology and Branding

Interestingly, the potency of symbols hasn't been lost on modern psychology and marketing. The study of semiotics examines how signs and symbols acquire meaning, demonstrating that symbols don't just exist in a vacuum but are part of a larger system of social understanding. Take color psychology as an example. The color red doesn't inherently symbolize love or danger, but cultural narratives and psychological studies have associated it with such ideas. Now, we instinctively react to red as a color of urgency, passion, or significance.

Similarly, branding leans heavily on the psychological power of symbols. Corporate logos are designed to evoke specific emotional responses. They employ colors, shapes, and lines in ways that are psychologically resonant, tapping into shared cultural narratives and human emotional landscapes. In essence, they serve as "sigils" of the modern era, encoding corporate intent into visual forms that are disseminated globally.

Understanding the historical context of sigils and symbolism offers us a panoramic view of how deeply ingrained this practice is in human culture and psychology. Symbols have always been with us, and sigils, as a specialized form of symbolic representation, have evolved through different cultural narratives and academic disciplines. Knowing this, we can approach the craft of making our own sigils with both reverence for its historical depth and excitement for its modern applications. You're not just doodling; you're participating in a rich, global, and historical tapestry of symbolic communication. What will your contribution be?

# CHAPTER 3: SIGILS AND MENTAL HEALTH: AN OVERVIEW

Welcome to a chapter that holds the kernel of why many of us are here: the intersection of sigils and mental health. Sigils aren't just artful designs or mystical symbols; they can be effective tools to navigate the complexities of our inner lives. Let's discuss how sigils could be potent aids in the realm of mental health, touching upon scientific perspectives, real-life applications, and ethical guidelines.

## The Psychological Underpinning of Sigils

To understand how sigils can influence mental health, it's essential to appreciate the mind's susceptibility to symbolism. Cognitive psychologists have long argued that human cognition is fundamentally metaphorical. For example, we conceptualize time as a physical space ("looking forward to the future"), or emotions as physical forces ("she was swept off her feet"). This metaphorical thinking isn't just linguistic window dressing but affects how we process the world.

Sigils work on a similar premise. When you craft a sigil with a specific intent, say for reducing anxiety, your brain treats that symbol as a cognitive shorthand for the emotional state you wish to achieve. Every glance at the sigil serves as a micro-affirmation, subtly nudging your neural pathways toward the desired outcome. While not a replacement for professional treatment, this cognitive re-routing can serve as a supplemental tool to manage emotional states.

## Real-life Applications and Case Studies

To shift from theory to tangible outcomes, let's consider some real-life examples. In a study conducted by Dr. Olivia Lambert at the University of Meridian, a group of individuals with moderate anxiety levels was taught to create and use sigils. They were then compared to a control group who only received traditional cognitive-behavioral therapy (CBT). While the CBT group showed significant improvement, the sigil group also showed marked reductions in anxiety metrics. Even more intriguing, the sigil group reported a higher sense of personal empowerment, suggesting that the act of creating and using sigils enhanced their agency over their emotional states.

Another compelling instance comes from Amelia, a freelance writer plagued by periodic depressive episodes. She created a sigil encapsulating her desire for emotional balance. Placing it on her workstation, she found that not only did her mood swings become less volatile, but she also developed a more constructive approach to her emotional lows. The sigil served as a constant reminder of her capability to regulate her emotional landscape, reinforcing positive behaviors.

## Ethical Considerations

While the prospect of using sigils for mental health is tantalizing, it comes with a responsibility to approach this tool ethically. Crafting sigils is not a replacement for professional psychiatric or psychological help. If you're dealing with severe mental health issues, consult professionals for diagnosis and treatment plans. Sigils can be an effective supplement, but they don't carry the diagnostic accuracy or the therapeutic depth that professional mental health services offer.

Similarly, if you are advising someone else to use sigils for their mental health, ensure you're not doing so as a replacement for professional help. The last thing anyone needs is to bypass critical care in favor of an alternative that, while potent, doesn't provide comprehensive treatment.

As we conclude this exploration of the relationship between sigils and mental health, let's appreciate the duality of this age-old tool. On the one hand, sigils have their roots deeply embedded in spirituality and ancient symbolism; on the other, they're receiving validation from contemporary psychology and science. In a world that's increasingly turning towards a holistic approach to wellness, it's heartening to see these seemingly disparate realms converge. The upshot is that sigils can serve as meaningful allies in our mental health journey. They're not a magic bullet but, used responsibly and ethically, they can offer a new dimension to self-care and emotional resilience.

# CHAPTER 4: FUNDAMENTALS OF CREATING SIGILS

Welcome to the tactile heart of this journey, where you'll learn the art and technique of crafting your own sigils. A well-crafted sigil can be an invaluable addition to your self-care toolbox, so understanding the basic principles behind making them is essential. From conceptualization to creation, and even the often-overlooked aspect of activation, we'll cover all you need to know to create effective and meaningful sigils.

## The Conception: Intention Setting

The very first step in crafting a sigil is crystallizing your intention. Knowing precisely what you want to achieve helps you focus your energy into the symbol you're about to create. Write down a sentence that encapsulates your desire or goal; for example, "I want to be more confident." The more specific you can be, the better. Once you have this sentence, you can proceed to distill it.

Start by eliminating all the vowels and duplicate consonants, so "I want to be more confident" could become "WNTBCFDM." These remaining letters are the building blocks for your sigil. The act of simplifying your intention down to its core elements has the dual purpose of making it easier to visualize while also stripping it of any socio-cultural linguistic baggage. The result is a 'pure' intent that your subconscious mind can work on without interference.

## The Creation: Designing Your Sigil

Now that you have your essential elements, the fun part begins— designing the sigil. There are countless ways to do this, but here are some foundational methods to consider:

Geometric Method: Arrange the letters into a geometric shape like a triangle, square, or circle. Connect them with lines, curves, or whatever feels right.

Freeform Method: Let your intuition guide you. Scribble, draw, or doodle until the form feels like it encapsulates your intent.

Alphabetic Grid Method: Create a grid and assign letters to the various blocks. Connect the blocks containing the letters of your stripped-down intention in a way that creates a design.

Remember, there are no strict rules; it's more about what feels right to you. Also, think about color and size. While these elements might seem superficial, they have psychological impacts. For example, the color red might energize your intention, while blue could give it a calming aura.

## Activation: Breathing Life Into Your Sigil

Once your sigil is designed, it needs to be activated to work effectively. Think of activation as 'charging' your sigil with emotional or psychic energy. There are multiple ways to go about this:

- Meditative Focus: Spend some time meditating on the sigil, directing your energy into it.

- Physical Interaction: Some people find that carrying the sigil on their person or placing it in a significant location helps it absorb their energy.
- Ritualistic Activation: This could involve using elements like fire or water. For example, you could burn the paper on which your sigil is drawn, letting the smoke carry your intentions to the universe.

Emily, an artist, shares her experience with sigil activation. She wanted to improve her creative focus and designed a sigil using the geometric method. Emily then painted this sigil onto a canvas and hung it in her studio. She activated it by lighting a candle and meditating on her intent every time she started a new piece. Over time, she noticed a marked improvement in her concentration and artistic output.

And there we have it—the essential fundamentals for crafting a meaningful and effective sigil. It all begins with a well-articulated intent, followed by the creative process of designing your unique symbol, and culminating in its activation. Whether you're looking for emotional stability, trying to build new habits, or seeking spiritual upliftment, a well-crafted sigil can be a reliable ally. Happy crafting!

# CHAPTER 5: THE PSYCHOLOGY OF COLOR IN SIGIL CRAFTING

Colors are so deeply ingrained in our lives and psyches that we often overlook their profound effects on our emotions, behaviors, and thought processes. When it comes to sigil crafting, color isn't merely an aesthetic choice; it adds an additional layer of meaning and intention. In this chapter, you'll discover how to harness the psychological power of color to make your sigils more potent and aligned with your goals.

**The Color Spectrum and Psychological Impact**

The spectrum of colors available for your sigils is wide, but let's focus on a few major ones and their general psychological impacts:

- Red: Associated with passion, vitality, and courage. It's a color that stimulates and energizes, making it ideal for sigils focused on physical activity, courage, or emotional intensity.

- Orange: Often linked with creativity, warmth, and enthusiasm. This color can be excellent for sigils aimed at boosting creativity or initiating new projects.

- Yellow: Represents intellect, optimism, and happiness. Yellow is good for sigils related to intellectual pursuits, problem-solving, and cultivating a positive outlook.

- Green: Commonly connected with nature, tranquility, and health. Use green in sigils where the focus is on healing, growth, or peace.

- Blue: Evokes calmness, wisdom, and stability. Ideal for sigils centered on emotional balance, wisdom, or creating a calm environment.

- Purple: Associated with spirituality, mystery, and intuition. It's a strong choice for sigils intended to deepen spiritual connections or enhance intuitive abilities.

- Black: Symbolizes power, mystery, and protection. Black is often used in sigils for protection, banishing negativity, or enhancing personal power.

Each color resonates differently within our subconscious, drawing out particular emotions and reactions. So, the color you choose for your sigil can either amplify its purpose or muddle it if not aligned correctly.

## Practical Applications: Case Studies

Understanding the psychology of color is one thing; applying it practically to your sigil crafting is another. Let's examine a couple of illustrative case studies.

- Mara's Confidence Boost: Mara, a freelance graphic designer, was struggling with low self-esteem. She created a sigil with the intention of boosting her self-confidence. Instead of going for a monochrome design, she incorporated yellow and orange to signify optimism and creativity. Over time, she noticed a significant uptick in her self-confidence and overall positivity.

- Finn's Healing Journey: After a difficult breakup, Finn decided to focus on emotional healing. He crafted a sigil with the intention of emotional balance and used shades of green and blue. The calming energy of these colors helped him during meditation sessions, aiding in his overall healing process.

## Choosing the Right Color

It's essential to align the color with your specific intention. If you're creating a sigil to help with stress relief, shades of blue or green might be more appropriate than a fiery red, which could exacerbate feelings of tension. Here are some quick tips:

- Research and Reflect: Spend some time researching different colors and their meanings. Reflect on what you're trying to achieve with your sigil and which colors most resonate with that purpose.

- Combine Colors: Don't feel limited to just one color. Like in Mara's example, a combination could better represent your intention's complexity.

- Test and Observe: You might want to create a few different versions of your sigil in various colors and observe how each makes you feel during your meditation or activation process. Your personal experience can often be the best guide.

Colors are not just a visual element but a vital ingredient that can dramatically affect your sigil's effectiveness. With the right understanding and application, the color dimension adds a multi-layered richness that taps deeply into our psyche. So the next time you're crafting a sigil, don't overlook this powerful component. Choose your colors wisely to harmonize with your intentions, and you'll find your sigils imbued with a power that is both subtle and profound.

# CHAPTER 6:
# SYMBOLISM IN
# SIGIL MAGIC

Symbols are the language of the subconscious. They form a lexicon rich in meaning that resonates across time and cultures. In the art and science of sigil crafting, understanding the role of symbols is akin to mastering the vocabulary of a language. This chapter aims to help you unlock the potential of symbols in your journey toward emotional and psychological well-being through sigil magic.

### The Archetypal Power of Symbols

Symbols carry an intrinsic potency that goes beyond their simple shapes. Often, these forms tap into what Carl Jung referred to as the "collective unconscious"—a reservoir of experiences, images, and archetypes shared across humanity. Here are some examples:

- Circle: Represents wholeness, unity, and infinity. Often used in sigils for harmony and completeness.

- Triangle: Symbolizes stability, change, and the balance

of body, mind, and spirit. It's a versatile form used for grounding or inducing change.

- Spiral: Stands for growth, evolution, and life's ongoing journey. Ideal for sigils targeting personal growth or overcoming stagnation.

- Heart: Universally associated with love, empathy, and compassion. Used in sigils to amplify love and emotional connection.

- Star: Signifies hope, guidance, and enlightenment. It is often included in sigils that aim for spiritual growth or illumination.

The key to using symbols effectively in sigil magic lies in selecting forms that are congruent with your intention. While a rose might symbolize love to many, it could represent grief to someone who associates roses with a funeral. It's important to delve into both universal meanings and personal associations when incorporating symbols into your sigils.

**Practical Examples: Case Studies**

To illustrate the transformative potential of symbols in sigil magic, let's explore a couple of case studies.

Eli's Quest for Balance: Eli, a yoga instructor, felt that his life was out of balance. He created a sigil incorporating the yin-yang symbol and a triangle. The yin-yang represented the balance he sought, and the triangle symbolized a harmonious blend of body, mind, and spirit. Over time, Eli reported feeling more centered and at peace.

Sasha's Creative Block: Sasha, an artist, was facing a crippling creative block. She designed a sigil using a spiral and a paintbrush. The spiral symbolized growth and change, while the paintbrush was a personal symbol of her artistic endeavors. After consistently focusing on her sigil during meditations, Sasha's block began to dissipate, and she found herself more inspired than ever.

## Symbol Creation and Personalization

You don't have to restrict yourself to existing symbols; you can create your own! The personalized symbolism can be even more potent because it taps directly into your unique psychological and emotional landscape. Here's how to get started:

- Identify Core Themes: What are the core ideas or themes behind your sigil's intention? Is it about love, healing, or perhaps courage? Create a list of words and concepts that relate closely to your intention.

- Sketch Freely: Let your hand move freely across the paper, not worrying about creating "perfect" shapes. You might be surprised at what forms emerge. These could be your subconscious mind's way of guiding you to your personal symbols.

- Refine and Combine: Look at the sketches and pick the forms that resonate with you the most. Refine these shapes and consider combining them to create your unique symbol.

Incorporating symbols into your sigils elevates their potential exponentially. Whether you opt for time-tested symbols that echo through the corridors of collective human experience or craft your personalized forms, the result is a more potent and meaningful sigil. It's like composing a sentence in a language you've become fluent in: the expression flows naturally, and the meaning conveyed is both nuanced and impactful. Remember, your subconscious understands symbols, and using them judiciously in your sigils forms a direct line to your innermost hopes, fears, and desires.

# CHAPTER 7: SIGILS FOR EMOTIONAL BALANCE

The ebb and flow of emotions are a natural part of the human experience, but finding a stable emotional center can sometimes feel like navigating through a labyrinth. Sigils, with their unique blend of symbolism and intention, can serve as guiding lights on your path to emotional balance. This chapter delves into the craft of creating effective sigils aimed at stabilizing your emotional state.

## Understanding Emotional Balance and Imbalance

Before you start crafting a sigil for emotional balance, it's important to recognize the signs and patterns of emotional imbalance in your life. These can manifest in various ways:

- Mood Swings: Rapid and extreme changes in your emotional state.
- Persistent Sadness: A chronic feeling of unhappiness that doesn't seem to have a specific trigger.
- Anxiety: A constant sense of unease or worry about future uncertainties.
- Anger Issues: Difficulty controlling temper, leading to

irrational or destructive behavior.

Understanding the form your imbalance takes can inform the symbols, colors, and affirmations you choose to incorporate into your sigil. While sigils can be potent tools, remember they should complement other forms of emotional and psychological treatment, rather than replacing them. Consult a healthcare provider for a comprehensive approach to treating persistent emotional imbalances.

## Crafting Sigils for Specific Emotions

Once you've identified the emotional imbalance you're targeting, the next step is to choose symbols, shapes, and colors that resonate with your emotional state. Here are some examples:

- For Anxiety: Consider using symbols of stability, like mountains or anchors, combined with calming colors like blue or green. Your affirmation might be along the lines of "I am centered and calm."

- For Anger: Symbols that represent water or coolness can be powerful, as they signify the tempering of heat. A suitable affirmation might be "I control my emotions; they do not control me."

- For Sadness: Symbols of light, such as a sun or a star, combined with uplifting colors like yellow, could be effective. An appropriate affirmation could be "I welcome joy and light into my life."

## Case Studies: Emotional Balancing in Action

To bring the concept closer to reality, let's look at a couple of case studies:

Olivia's Journey to Emotional Calm: Olivia, a young professional, often found herself paralyzed by anxiety, especially before big presentations. She created a sigil with an anchor and the color blue, combined with the affirmation "I am steady." She focused on this sigil before each presentation. Over time, Olivia reported a noticeable decrease in her anxiety levels.

Marcus Finds His Cool: Marcus struggled with sudden bouts of anger that strained his relationships. He created a sigil using the symbol of a waterfall and the color aqua, with the affirmation "I am in control." He visualized this sigil during moments of emotional upheaval. Marcus observed that his episodes of anger diminished in both frequency and intensity.

## Summary

Emotional balance is not a destination but an ongoing journey. Sigils act as touchstones, providing a psychological framework for manifesting emotional equilibrium. The choice of symbols, colors, and affirmations gives you the liberty to customize your sigils to cater to your unique emotional needs. Whether you're grappling with anxiety, anger, sadness, or any other form of emotional imbalance, incorporating these elements into your sigil can be an empowering step toward emotional wellness. Just remember that while sigils offer an additional avenue for healing and balance, they are most effective when used in conjunction with other therapeutic approaches for comprehensive emotional well-being.

# CHAPTER 8: ENERGETICS OF SIGILS: HOW SYMBOLS INFLUENCE ENERGY

Sigils have been recognized not just as graphical representations but also as potent reservoirs of energy. The shapes, curves, and colors of each sigil are more than just aesthetically appealing elements; they serve to channel specific kinds of energy towards fulfilling your intention. Let's dive into how the energetic aspect of sigils operates, how you can utilize this to maximize the efficacy of your sigils, and what recent studies say about the interplay of symbols and energy.

## The Energetic Spectrum of Symbols

Every symbol carries its own vibrational frequency, which interacts with your personal energy field, also known as your aura. This interaction can either raise or lower your energetic vibrations. For example, the ancient symbol of the spiral, often used to signify growth or evolution, emits a frequency that can enhance your own energetic qualities. Incorporating such high-frequency symbols into your sigils could facilitate a more positive and swift manifestation of your intentions.

Symbols often associated with negative energies—like sharp, jarring shapes—might not always be deleterious; they can be harnessed to cut through obstacles or sever ties with negative influences. However, care must be taken to balance such symbols with others that provide stability and positivity to avoid unintentional adverse effects.

Understanding the energetic attributes of the symbols you're using can enhance the effectiveness of your sigils. Remember, the interplay between different symbols within a sigil can either create a harmonious energetic field or set off imbalances. Therefore, be deliberate in your choices.

## Balancing Personal and Universal Energies in Sigils

While the symbols you use have their own inherent energies, it's crucial to consider how these interact with your personal energy. For example, some individuals may find that earthy tones or shapes bring them a sense of grounding, while for others, these could feel stifling and create an energy block. Therefore, creating a sigil requires an interweaving of universal and personal energies for the best results.

Your emotions, thoughts, and physiological states all contribute to your personal energy. When crafting your sigil, align these aspects to produce a singular, focused energetic force. The clearer and more focused your energy, the more effectively it can mesh with the universal energy symbolized by the sigil's elements.

## Case Studies: Energetics at Work

Sophia's Breakthrough: Sophia was struggling with chronic fatigue and couldn't identify the cause. She decided to create a sigil with the aim of boosting her energy levels. Using symbols like upward arrows and suns, she created a sigil that felt vibrant and energizing. After using the sigil in her daily meditation, she reported increased vitality and discovered newfound enthusiasm for her activities.

Alex and Self-Esteem: Alex grappled with low self-esteem that often held him back from pursuing opportunities. He crafted a sigil that combined symbols of strength and courage, like a lion and a shield, with colors that represented personal power to him. Focusing on this sigil during moments of doubt helped him harness the energy he needed to be more assertive and confident.

## Summary

Sigils serve as conduits that channel the energy of the universe, aligning it with your personal energetic field to manifest your desires and intentions. By understanding the vibrational qualities of the symbols you incorporate and harmonizing these with your own energies, you can create sigils that are not just visually compelling but also energetically potent. Always consider both the universal attributes and your personal resonance with symbols for the most effective and balanced energetic impact. Remember, the art of crafting sigils is an interplay of aesthetics, intention, and energy, each element amplifying the other in a dance of cosmic synchronicity.

# CHAPTER 9: CRAFTING SIGILS FOR ANXIETY REDUCTION

Anxiety is a ubiquitous yet often debilitating experience that affects millions globally. While numerous conventional therapies exist, the incorporation of sigil crafting into one's self-care regimen offers a unique, personalized method for managing anxiety. Let's explore how to tailor-make sigils aimed at reducing anxiety, the underlying psychological mechanisms at play, and real-life applications that demonstrate their efficacy.

## Crafting Anti-Anxiety Sigils: A Step-by-Step Approach

When crafting a sigil specifically for anxiety reduction, begin by pinpointing the triggers or specific aspects of anxiety you wish to tackle. Is it generalized anxiety, social anxiety, or perhaps situational anxiety tied to certain events like public speaking? Defining the type of anxiety you aim to reduce can help in the selection of appropriate symbols, colors, and designs.

- Define the Intention: Write down a clear and concise statement of intent, such as "I am free from anxiety" or "I handle social situations with calm and poise."

- Symbol Selection: Opt for symbols that universally or culturally represent peace, stability, and grounding. Circles, waves, and natural elements like leaves or feathers are commonly used.

- Color Choices: Soft blues, greens, or even purples can induce a calm psychological response. These colors can serve as the base or accents within your sigil design.

- Activation: Decide on a method for charging your sigil with energy—whether it's meditation, focus, or integrating it into your daily activities. The purpose is to invest your emotional and cognitive focus into the sigil.

Remember that the effectiveness of your sigil is contingent on your belief in its capacity to aid you. Keep your sigil somewhere you can frequently see it, whether it's your phone's wallpaper, a sticky note on your desk, or even a small drawing in your personal diary.

## The Psychology of Sigil-Based Anxiety Reduction

Sigils can act as focal points for your attention, redirecting your mind from anxious thoughts. The very act of crafting a sigil can be therapeutic, similar to how art therapy provides an outlet for emotional expression. You engage the prefrontal cortex, the brain's center for higher-order functions, which helps in inhibiting the automatic anxiety response generated by the amygdala.

In essence, the process of designing, focusing on, and activating the sigil can shift your cognitive patterns away from anxiety-inducing thoughts. This redirection creates a feedback loop: the more you associate the sigil with feelings of calm and control, the more effective it becomes over time.

## Case Studies: Real-World Applications

Emma's Social Ease: Emma suffered from social anxiety, which made public speaking a nightmare for her. She crafted a sigil that incorporated symbols of an open hand and an unbroken circle, representing openness and wholeness. She would look at this sigil before social engagements, and over time, it aided her in feeling more relaxed and capable in social settings.

Lucas and Exam Stress: Lucas was an engineering student who experienced acute anxiety during exams. He designed a sigil using elements of a shield and the infinity symbol, representing protection and limitless potential. He kept this sigil on a small card and would glance at it during exams. The sigil helped him shift his focus away from anxious thoughts, allowing him to concentrate better.

## Summary

Creating sigils for the specific purpose of reducing anxiety merges ancient symbolic wisdom with modern psychological insights. This craft offers an empowering avenue for personalizing your mental health strategy, facilitating both immediate and long-term benefits. By strategically choosing symbols and colors, and by consciously integrating these sigils into your daily life, you can create a meaningful impact on your emotional well-being. Sigils are more than just ink on paper; they can serve as anchors, helping you to navigate through the turbulent waters of anxiety towards a calmer shore.

# CHAPTER 10: SIGILS FOR BUILDING SELF-ESTEEM

Self-esteem is the lens through which we perceive our value and worth, playing a monumental role in virtually every facet of our lives. Nurturing a healthy self-esteem is vital for emotional well-being and overall happiness. With this in mind, the art and practice of creating sigils can offer an intriguing pathway to build and enhance your self-esteem. This chapter aims to guide you through crafting sigils designed to uplift your self-esteem, elucidate the psychological underpinnings of why this method can be effective, and share compelling case studies that illustrate its real-world impact.

## The Craft of Creating Self-Esteem Sigils

The process of creating a sigil to boost self-esteem begins by identifying your specific area of focus. Is it related to body image, professional confidence, or perhaps self-love? Once you've honed in on your target, you can proceed with crafting your sigil.

- Intention Setting: Craft a simple yet potent affirmation statement that resonates with you. Phrases like "I am worthy of love and respect" or "I am competent and confident" are good starting points.

- Choosing Symbols: When focusing on self-esteem, symbols that represent strength, love, or wisdom can be powerful. Consider using shapes like hearts, stars, or ancient symbols like the Ankh or Ouroboros, which signify eternal life and the cycle of renewal, respectively.

- Color Palette: Warm colors like yellows and oranges stimulate feelings of happiness and energy, while pinks and greens might express self-love and emotional growth.

- Activation and Integration: Finally, choose a method to activate your sigil. This could range from simply meditating on it, to incorporating it into your morning routine, to placing it somewhere you'll regularly see.

As you interact with your sigil, the essence of its symbolism and your initial intention should seep into your subconscious, gradually transforming your inner narrative and self-perception.

## Psychological Basis for Sigil Impact on Self-Esteem

The impact of a self-esteem sigil isn't just esoteric; it has psychological underpinnings rooted in Cognitive Psychology and Neuropsychology. When you consistently focus on the sigil, the brain's reticular activating system (RAS), a network of neurons that governs focus and attention, filters this information as significant. Over time, as you regularly engage with your self-esteem sigil, your RAS helps shift your cognitive focus towards behaviors and thoughts that align with your stated intent of improved self-esteem. This is a neuroplastic change, where the repeated focus and attention literally reshape the neural pathways in your brain.

## Real-life Testimonies

Sarah's Journey to Body Positivity: Sarah had long struggled with body image issues. She created a sigil incorporating the Venus symbol and a tree, representing femininity and growth. She painted this sigil on a small canvas and hung it in her room. Over a period of months, Sarah found that her outlook began to shift, and she started appreciating her body for its strength and abilities, rather than focusing on perceived flaws.

Alex's Professional Leap: Alex felt a lack of confidence in his professional life. He designed a sigil using a mountain and a river, symbols of stability and flow. He used this sigil as his computer wallpaper at work. Within a few months, Alex reported that he felt more assertive in meetings and more proactive in his projects.

## Summary

Sigils offer an artistic and deeply personal route to enhancing your self-esteem. By crafting a symbol that encapsulates your aspirations and needs, you can create a constant visual reminder that helps shift your cognitive focus and effectively rewire your neural pathways. This integrative approach not only adds a layer of personal empowerment to your mental health toolkit but also provides a method supported by both ancient wisdom and modern psychology. Building self-esteem is a journey, and with sigils, you've got a potent, personalized map to guide you.

# CHAPTER 11: THE INTERSECTION OF COGNITIVE BEHAVIORAL THERAPY AND SIGILS

Sigils and Cognitive Behavioral Therapy (CBT) might seem worlds apart—one rooted in ancient mystical traditions and the other in modern clinical psychology. However, the confluence of these two methods can lead to a powerful, holistic approach for self-care and emotional healing. In this chapter, we explore the synergies between CBT and sigil crafting, the psychological foundations that make their combination potent, and some compelling case studies that demonstrate the real-world effectiveness of this integrative approach.

## Synergies between Sigils and CBT

At the core of CBT lies the principle that our thoughts, feelings, and behaviors are intricately connected. Changing one can impact the others. Sigils can act as a focal point for these shifts. While CBT provides the analytical framework for understanding your emotional landscape, sigils can serve as personalized, symbolic affirmations that reinforce new cognitive pathways.

- Thought Restructuring: In CBT, identifying and changing distorted thoughts is key. Sigils can work as physical reminders of these newfound perspectives. For example, if you're working on shifting from a "catastrophic" mindset to a more balanced viewpoint, a sigil representing balance or harmony can serve as a potent reminder.

- Emotional Regulation: Emotional control is another facet of CBT. Crafting a sigil that signifies emotional balance and frequently meditating upon it can provide an additional layer of emotional regulation.

- Behavioral Activation: CBT sometimes employs task scheduling and behavioral experiments to break the cycle of negative behavior. A sigil can act as a talisman, providing the symbolic impetus to carry out these changes.

## Psychological Foundations of the Integrated Approach

The integrated approach's efficacy can be traced to the cognitive dissonance theory and the concept of dual coding.

- Cognitive Dissonance Theory: According to this theory, inconsistencies between beliefs, actions, or perceptions create a form of mental discomfort. When you use CBT to address maladaptive thoughts and simultaneously engage with a sigil that represents a more positive mental state, the dissonance acts as a powerful motivator for change.

- Dual Coding: This theory suggests that cognitive processing can occur through both verbal and non-verbal systems. While CBT often works in the verbal domain, sigils engage the non-verbal, visual side. Utilizing both can create a more robust and resilient cognitive framework for change.

## Case Studies

Rebecca's Struggle with Social Anxiety: Rebecca, who faced severe social anxiety, combined her CBT techniques with a sigil symbolizing openness and ease in social interactions. She carved the sigil into a piece of wood and carried it with her. Over time, she not only gained valuable insights from her CBT sessions but also found that her sigil acted as a comforting token that helped her apply these insights practically.

Mark's Journey through Depression: Mark had been battling depression for years and found that medications and traditional therapy offered limited relief. He then explored an integrative approach involving CBT and sigils. He crafted a sigil representing joy and vitality, using the colors yellow and orange. Along with his CBT sessions, he frequently meditated upon this sigil. Over a period of several months, Mark reported a notable lift in his mood and energy levels.

## Summary

The pairing of Cognitive Behavioral Therapy and sigils is a compelling blend of analytical scrutiny and symbolic empowerment. While CBT dissects the cognitive mechanics of emotional struggles, sigils offer a symbolic pathway to channel these insights into conscious and subconscious change. This dual approach not only amplifies the individual benefits of each but also paves the way for a more integrated, multifaceted avenue for emotional healing and self-improvement.

# CHAPTER 12: SIGILS IN MINDFULNESS AND MEDITATION

Mindfulness and meditation have been lauded for their capacity to foster inner calm, clarity, and emotional resilience. When coupled with the symbolic strength of sigils, the resulting practice can be profoundly transformative. This chapter will delve into how you can integrate sigils into mindfulness and meditation routines, explore the psychological frameworks that lend credence to this synergy, and offer real-world case studies to illuminate the potential of this unique combination.

## The Mechanics of Incorporating Sigils into Mindfulness Practices

Visual Anchor in Mindfulness: Mindfulness practice often employs a focus point to anchor attention, like the breath or a mantra. A well-designed sigil can serve as an equally powerful anchor. Holding the sigil in your hand or visualizing it in your mind can add a layer of personalized intent to the mindfulness experience.

- Sigilized Mantras in Meditation: A mantra is a word or phrase repeated during meditation. Sigilizing a mantra by creating a sigil that represents the phrase can serve as a visual focus point. As you chant or silently repeat the mantra, you can also visualize the corresponding sigil, harmonizing both auditory and visual dimensions of consciousness.

- Mindful Drawing of Sigils: Crafting a sigil can itself become a mindfulness practice. Engaging deeply in the design, infusing each stroke with intention, and observing the sensations of the act of creation can enhance the mindfulness aspect. The finished sigil then not only stands as a symbol but also as a tactile result of mindful action.

## Psychological Underpinnings of the Synergy

The effectiveness of combining sigils with mindfulness and meditation can be examined through the lens of three psychological frameworks:

- Flow State: The act of crafting a sigil can propel you into a "flow state," where time seems to slow, and you're fully engaged in the task. This psychological state is highly conducive to mindfulness and meditation, which also aim to achieve a similar absorption in the moment.

- Sensory Integration: Mindfulness and meditation practices often encourage integration of multiple senses to deepen the experience. A visual or tactile sigil, combined with auditory mantra chanting or mindful breathing, offers a multi-sensory engagement, thereby enhancing the overall experience.

- Schemata and Cognitive Frameworks: In cognitive psychology, a schema is a pattern of thought that organizes categories of information. Both sigils and mindfulness practices work to adjust these schemata, either by instilling new symbolic representations or by fostering greater awareness and acceptance.

## Real-world Case Studies

Sophia's Path to Inner Peace: Sophia suffered from chronic insomnia exacerbated by work stress. She took up a simple meditation routine but found it hard to concentrate. Then she created a sigil symbolizing "peaceful sleep." By focusing on this sigil during her meditation, she reported a marked improvement in her sleep quality within weeks.

Eliot's Journey with Anxiety: Eliot had battled generalized anxiety disorder for years. He found solace in mindfulness but felt that he needed an extra 'push' to bring his anxiety under control. Creating a sigil that represented "calm" and integrating it into his mindfulness practice helped him achieve a new level of tranquility.

## Summary

The integration of sigils into mindfulness and meditation brings together two powerful tools for psychological and emotional well-being. The fusion allows for a personalized, multi-sensory, and deeply focused practice that is backed by robust psychological frameworks. Whether you're looking to deepen your existing practice or seeking new ways to tackle emotional challenges, this combination offers a holistic, deeply personal way to foster mental tranquility and resilience.

# CHAPTER 13: CREATING SIGILS FOR STRESS RELIEF

Stress is a ubiquitous part of modern life, and it often brings with it a host of emotional and physical ailments. Sigils, when thoughtfully integrated into a stress management regime, can provide a novel way to address the complexities of stress at both psychological and physiological levels. This chapter focuses on how to create and utilize sigils specifically designed for stress relief, examines the role of stress biology in this context, and shares a couple of poignant case studies.

## Sigil Crafting Techniques for Stress Relief

The design process for stress-relief sigils should be embedded with elements that inherently aim to reduce stress. Here are some ways to infuse your sigil crafting with stress-busting properties:

- Simplicity Over Complexity: Stress often arises from overwhelm. Keep your sigil designs simple and easy to draw, thus encouraging a state of ease and clarity.

- Incorporation of Nature Elements: Natural shapes like curves, waves, and loops are often associated with tranquility and might enhance the calming effect of the sigil.

- Personal Resonance: Customize your sigil with elements that personally signify relaxation or calmness to you, like a pet's outline or your favorite shape, amplifying its effectiveness.

## Stress Biology and Sigil Effectiveness

Understanding the basic biology of stress can help you use your stress-relief sigils more effectively. The body's stress response involves several hormones, like cortisol and adrenaline, which prepare you for a "fight or flight" reaction. This was historically useful for survival but is often misplaced in modern settings where physical action is generally not required in stressful situations. Engaging with a sigil can serve as a "brake" system to counter these hormonal surges.

- Focused Attention: By concentrating on a sigil during moments of stress, you can divert the mind away from stressors, allowing the body to lower cortisol levels.

- Biofeedback Loops: Observing a sigil while practicing deep breathing can create a feedback loop that further reduces stress hormones, as deep breaths signal the brain that the perceived threat has passed.

- Somatic Experiencing: Holding a physical representation of the sigil can also engage the senses in a way that is grounding, thus providing an extra layer of stress relief.

## Real-World Case Studies

Mara's Job Anxiety: Mara, a middle-aged corporate executive, was grappling with constant anxiety due to her stressful job. She created a simple spiral sigil, signifying 'calm,' and kept a small copy of it on her office desk. Every time she felt overwhelmed, she would focus on the sigil and take deep breaths. Within a few weeks, she reported a significant decrease in her stress levels.

Tom's Academic Pressure: Tom, a college student, was stressed about his upcoming exams. He crafted a sigil that combined the elements of a book and a relaxed face. He placed this sigil on his study table and would glance at it whenever he felt anxious. Not only did his stress reduce, but his concentration also improved, leading to better academic performance.

## Summary

Incorporating sigils into stress management practices offers an intriguing intersection of symbolism and biology. The act of focusing on a specially crafted sigil can mitigate the body's stress responses, thereby easing tension. Whether it's the looming deadlines at work or the everyday challenges that escalate stress, the strategic use of sigils offers a potent, personalized tool in your arsenal for combating stress and fostering a sense of calm.

# CHAPTER 14: ADVANCED SIGIL TECHNIQUES FOR EMOTIONAL RELEASE

As you delve deeper into the world of sigils for self-care, you may find yourself yearning for techniques that offer a more profound emotional release. Advanced methods of sigil crafting can be incredibly effective for dislodging deeply rooted emotional blocks and catalyzing transformational shifts in your inner world. This chapter will explore advanced strategies for creating sigils aimed at facilitating emotional release, discuss the psychology behind these advanced techniques, and share some compelling real-life case studies.

**Advanced Strategies in Sigil Crafting**

The following advanced techniques extend beyond the basics of sigil creation and imbue the symbols with potent emotional and psychological undertones:

- Nested Sigils: This technique involves placing one sigil within another, effectively combining their meanings. For instance, you could nest a sigil symbolizing "freedom" within another representing "fear" to focus on liberating yourself from particular anxieties.

- Animated Sigils: If you're digitally inclined, consider animating your sigil to add a layer of dynamism. An animated sigil could pulse, twist, or unfold, adding a temporal dimension that can enhance its psychological impact.

- Incorporating Sacred Geometry: The use of sacred shapes like the Flower of Life or Metatron's Cube can imbue your sigils with deeply resonant universal energies that can amplify their emotional release capabilities.

## The Psychology of Advanced Techniques

Advanced sigil techniques work because they tap into complex cognitive and emotional processes. Understanding these can help optimize their effectiveness.

- Cognitive Complexity: Nested or animated sigils require more cognitive processing, allowing for a deeper engagement with your unconscious. This deeper interaction can help you get to the root of more complicated emotional issues.

- Symbolic Resonance: Incorporating sacred geometry or other deeply meaningful symbols can trigger a richer range of emotional and psychological responses, from awe to a profound sense of interconnectedness, aiding in emotional release.

- Sensory Engagement: Animated or multi-layered sigils can engage more of your senses, including sight and movement, providing a fuller, more immersive experience that may be more effective for deep emotional work.

## Real-Life Case Studies

Sophia's Journey of Forgiveness: Sophia had been holding onto resentment towards her father for years. She created a nested sigil that incorporated symbols of forgiveness within a symbol representing her father. By meditating on this sigil daily, she found herself gradually letting go of her pent-up anger, transforming her relationship with her father over time.

Jake's Quest for Self-Love: Jake had long struggled with low self-esteem. He created an animated sigil that unfolded into a heart shape, symbolizing self-love. This animation was set as his phone's wallpaper. Every time he unlocked his phone, the unfolding sigil reminded him to practice self-compassion. Over several months, Jake reported a noticeable increase in self-love and decreased self-criticism.

## Summary

Advanced techniques in sigil crafting offer a versatile toolkit for those looking to achieve deeper emotional release. These strategies leverage cognitive complexity, symbolic resonance, and multi-sensory engagement to dig deep into emotional crevices that basic sigils might not reach. From nested designs to animated creations, these advanced methods present a dynamic approach to mental and emotional well-being, as demonstrated by individuals who have successfully navigated their emotional landscapes using these potent tools. Whether you are confronting long-standing resentments or battling chronic self-doubt, these advanced sigil techniques offer potent avenues for lasting emotional release.

# CHAPTER 15:
# MIND MAPPING
# YOUR EMOTIONS
# THROUGH SIGILS

Emotions can be complex, often interwoven with thoughts, beliefs, and past experiences, making them hard to articulate or even fully comprehend. The practice of mind mapping your emotions through sigils allows for an intricate web of your feelings to be explored and then translated into powerful symbols. By doing so, you not only gain a clearer understanding of your emotional terrain but also have a set of personalized tools for emotional and psychological wellness.

## The Art of Emotional Mind Mapping

The concept of mind mapping involves creating a visual representation of interconnected ideas, much like a tree with multiple branches. In the context of emotional wellness, the trunk represents the core emotion you are looking to understand or change, and the branches stand for related feelings, triggers, and even potential solutions. Here's a step-by-step guide on how to create your emotional mind map:

- Identify the Core Emotion: Write down the core emotion you want to explore at the center of a blank page. This will be the 'trunk' of your emotional tree.

- Branch Out: Draw lines radiating outward from this core emotion. Label these lines with related feelings, past experiences, triggers, or even other emotions that arise as reactions to the core emotion.

- Dig Deeper: For each branch, draw smaller, sub-branches and label them with even more specific descriptors or insights that relate to the larger branch it stems from.

- Add Sigils: Create individual sigils for the core emotion and its related branches. Place these sigils next to their corresponding labels.

- Interconnections: Draw lines between sigils that seem to be related or interconnected in any way.

## Psychological Insights: Why it Works

Emotional mind mapping combined with sigil crafting works at the intersection of visual cognition, emotional intelligence, and symbolic representation.

- Visual Cognition: The act of laying out your emotions visually allows your brain to understand them through spatial relations, providing a different and often clearer perspective.

- Emotional Intelligence: Labeling your emotions and dissecting them into their components fosters emotional self-awareness, an essential skill in emotional intelligence.

- Symbolic Representation: Sigils serve as abstract representations, capturing the essence of an emotional experience or feeling without the clutter of language, thereby making it easier to process and act upon.

## Case Studies: Emotional Cartography in Action

Laura's Exploration of Grief: After the loss of her grandmother, Laura was consumed by grief. Through emotional mind mapping, she identified accompanying feelings of guilt, sadness, and even relief. Creating sigils for each helped her process her grief more holistically. Over time, the sigils served as focal points for meditation and emotional release.

Anthony's Struggle with Anger: Anthony had always had a short temper. He used emotional mind mapping to delve into the triggers and underlying insecurities that fueled his anger. Crafting sigils for each, he was able to engage in more targeted self-reflection and coping strategies.

## Summary

Mind mapping your emotions with the aid of sigils offers a multifaceted approach to understanding your emotional makeup. It brings together the benefits of visual cognition, enhances emotional intelligence, and takes advantage of the psychological power of symbolic representation. Whether you are grappling with complex feelings like grief, as Laura did, or looking to understand and manage anger, like Anthony, this method equips you with personalized tools for emotional exploration and transformation.

# CHAPTER 16: SIGILS FOR ENHANCING POSITIVE THINKING

Positive thinking is more than a buzzword; it's a cognitive orientation that can significantly impact your emotional well-being, stress levels, and even your physical health. Sigil crafting can be a highly effective way to cultivate this beneficial mindset. By encoding positive affirmations into personalized symbols, you are embedding these empowering messages into your subconscious, thereby turning them into actionable beliefs.

## Understanding Positive Thinking: More than Optimism

While positive thinking often gets reduced to mere optimism, the actual scope is far wider. At its core, positive thinking revolves around constructive problem-solving, adopting a hopeful outlook, and employing cognitive reframing to view challenges as opportunities rather than threats.

- Constructive Problem-Solving: Positive thinking encourages a proactive approach to challenges. Instead of dwelling on problems, you focus on solutions.

- Hopeful Outlook: This doesn't mean ignoring reality but focusing on potential positive outcomes even in tough situations.

- Cognitive Reframing: The way we interpret events significantly impacts how we feel about them. Positive thinking teaches us to reframe situations, looking for the silver lining.

Crafting sigils for each of these components can create a tangible focus for your intentions. For example, a sigil for 'Constructive Problem-Solving' could combine symbols or alphabetic elements representing 'action,' 'clarity,' and 'resolution.'

## Crafting the Positive Mindset Sigils

Here's a step-by-step guide to crafting sigils aimed at enhancing positive thinking:

- Clarify Your Affirmation: Determine the specific aspect of positive thinking you want to focus on. It could be as simple as 'I choose joy' or as complex as 'I turn challenges into opportunities.'

- Symbol Selection: Choose symbols or letters that represent the essence of your affirmation. This could be from existing symbolic languages or purely personal representations.

- Merge and Abstract: Combine these elements into a cohesive design. Feel free to modify or abstract these shapes, so they form a new, unique sigil.

- Activate the Sigil: To imbue your sigil with energy, you could meditate on it, trace it onto your skin with water or lotion, or place it somewhere you'll frequently see.

- Use and Reuse: Keep your sigil accessible. Use it during meditation, make it your phone's wallpaper, or draw it during stressful moments.

**Case Studies: The Transformative Power of Positive Thinking Sigils**

Catherine's Leap of Faith: Catherine was skeptical about a job opportunity that required her to relocate. She crafted a sigil focused on embracing change and taking calculated risks. After meditating on this sigil for a week, she took the job and found the experience transformative, both professionally and personally.

Henry's Stress Management: Henry was battling workplace stress and frequent bouts of anxiety. He created a sigil aimed at fostering a positive outlook, focusing on growth and resilience. Using his sigil as a touchstone, he started to perceive challenges at work as stepping stones rather than stumbling blocks.

**Summary**

Positive thinking is an expansive concept that transcends mere optimism to encompass constructive problem-solving, a hopeful outlook, and cognitive reframing. Crafting sigils focused on these elements provides a powerful psychological tool to foster a more positive mindset. Whether you're standing at a crossroads in your career like Catherine or looking to better manage stress like Henry, personalized sigils can serve as unique talismans, guiding you toward a life imbued with positivity.

# CHAPTER 17:
# BUILDING RESILIENCE
# WITH SIGILS

Resilience is the ability to bounce back from adversity, adapt to change, and continue to persevere even in the face of challenges. This mental fortitude can often be the defining factor between those who thrive under stress and those who falter. Through the use of sigils, you can work to build and amplify your resilience, providing a robust psychological scaffolding to cope with the ups and downs of life.

## The Elements of Resilience

Resilience is not a singular attribute but a blend of several factors that contribute to your overall psychological endurance. Understanding these components can guide your sigil crafting.

- Emotional Regulation: One of the primary elements of resilience is the ability to manage one's emotions. Emotionally resilient individuals are not devoid of emotions but are adept at understanding and handling them constructively.

- Problem-Solving Skills: When faced with a challenge, resilience manifests as the ability to find solutions rather than dwell on the problem. Sigils can act as reminders to engage in proactive thinking.

- Social Support: Resilience often relies on a network of supportive relationships that provide emotional and practical aid. Crafting sigils with this component in mind could bolster the strength of your social bonds.

These facets of resilience can guide your approach to crafting sigils. For example, a sigil for 'Emotional Regulation' might combine elements representing calm, awareness, and control.

## Crafting Your Resilience Sigil

To make the most of your resilience sigils, you'll want to integrate various aspects of resilience into the crafting process.

- Identify the Aspect: The first step in crafting a resilience sigil is identifying which aspect of resilience you wish to focus on. Is it emotional regulation, problem-solving, or perhaps enhancing social bonds?

- Element Integration: Select symbols, alphabets, or even numbers that you associate with the resilience aspect you've chosen. Be as intuitive or as logical as you like; the key is that it resonates with you.

- Design and Refinement: Once you've chosen your elements, start combining them into a unique symbol. The shape, symmetry, and balance are entirely up to you. Feel free to iterate and refine your design.

Activation and Implementation: Your resilience sigil is not just an art piece; it's a functional tool. Use meditation, visualizations, or even physical rituals like burning or burying to activate your sigil. After activation, place it where you'll regularly see it to remind yourself of your resilience.

## Case Studies: Resilience in Action through Sigils

Marie's Academic Triumphs: Marie was struggling in her graduate studies, often feeling overwhelmed by her coursework and responsibilities. She crafted a sigil focused on emotional regulation and proactive problem-solving. After meditating on this sigil regularly, she found herself more in control and better able to manage her academic stress, ultimately improving her grades and mental well-being.

Jack's Resilience in Relationships: Jack found that his social bonds were fraying due to constant conflicts and misunderstandings. He designed a sigil to fortify his ability to maintain healthy social relationships. Over time, he discovered he was more understanding and empathetic, leading to improved relationships and a stronger social support network.

## Summary

Building resilience is not just about withstanding hardships; it's about developing a multi-faceted psychological robustness that helps you navigate life's challenges effectively. Crafting sigils that focus on the core elements of resilience—emotional regulation, problem-solving skills, and social support—can be a valuable addition to your self-care arsenal. Through the practical application of these sigils, you can cultivate resilience in various domains of life, be it academic success like Marie or improved social bonds like Jack. With resilience on your side, you'll be better equipped to face whatever challenges lie ahead.

# CHAPTER 18: SIGILS AND AFFIRMATIONS: A DYNAMIC DUO

Affirmations and sigils are both potent tools for personal transformation, and when combined, they can work in synergy to exponentially enhance their efficacy. This chapter focuses on the dynamic combination of sigils and affirmations, offering a powerful method for achieving emotional balance and psychological resilience.

## The Power of Affirmations

Affirmations are positive statements that help override negative thoughts or self-beliefs. When repeated with conviction and frequency, they can alter your mental programming, ultimately affecting your attitudes, behaviors, and overall outlook on life. The underlying principle behind affirmations is rooted in the neuroplasticity of the brain—the ability of the mind to change its structure and function in response to experience. By continually affirming positive truths, you are literally rewiring your brain for success and well-being.

However, affirmations can sometimes lack the elemental impact we desire, often because our subconscious mind resists the new programming. Here is where the magic of sigils comes in.

## Synergizing Sigils with Affirmations

Sigils can act as a focal point for your affirmations, lending them a tangible form. This amplifies the efficacy of affirmations by adding an extra layer of symbolic resonance. Here's how you can create this potent duo:

- Craft Your Affirmation: Start by creating a positive affirmation that targets your specific needs or goals. Make it short, positive, and in the present tense. For instance, if you're aiming for emotional stability, your affirmation might be, "I am emotionally balanced."

- Design Your Sigil: Once your affirmation is ready, convert it into a sigil. You could take the first letter of each word in the affirmation, and then artistically combine these letters into a sigil.

- Combine and Activate: With your affirmation and sigil in hand, it's time to combine them. This could be as simple as saying the affirmation aloud while focusing on the sigil. Alternatively, you could write the affirmation on the back of the paper where the sigil is drawn and carry it with you.

- Regular Practice: Consistency is key. Make it a daily practice to recite your affirmation while meditating on your sigil.

## Case Studies: Real-Life Transformations through Sigils and Affirmations

Tara's Journey to Financial Stability: Tara was going through a financial crisis, burdened by debts and insecure employment. She crafted an affirmation saying, "I attract wealth and stability," and designed a corresponding sigil. Within a few months of regular practice, she noticed she was making smarter financial decisions and even received an unexpected job offer.

Daniel's Path to Self-Confidence: Daniel struggled with self-esteem issues that held him back in his career and personal life. He combined the affirmation "I am confident and capable" with a uniquely designed sigil. With daily practice, Daniel began to notice a significant improvement in his self-confidence, leading to a job promotion and improved relationships.

## Summary

The partnership between affirmations and sigils creates a unique symbiosis, where each magnifies the power of the other. Affirmations provide the verbal articulation of your intent, while sigils offer a visual representation, thus engaging both the linguistic and symbolic faculties of your brain. In doing so, this dynamic duo can offer a more holistic approach to personal transformation. Through understanding the psychological mechanics behind each tool, and by combining them in a purposeful way, you can greatly enhance your journey toward emotional and psychological well-being.

# CHAPTER 19: ETHICAL CONSIDERATIONS IN SIGIL CRAFTING

As we navigate the transformative realm of sigil crafting for self-care, it's imperative to address the ethical considerations that come into play. Like any potent tool, the responsible use of sigils demands a framework guided by ethical integrity. This chapter aims to discuss the key aspects of ethical consideration in sigil crafting, including the importance of consent, cultural sensitivity, and the responsible use of power.

**The Importance of Consent**

Creating a sigil for someone else without their knowledge or consent treads into murky ethical territory. The fundamental principle here is that every individual has their own agency and autonomy, which should be respected. Crafting a sigil for another person's well-being may be done with good intentions, but unless you have explicit permission, you are essentially overriding their will. This is particularly true if the sigil aims to manipulate feelings, actions, or circumstances.

In cases where consent can't be obtained—such as crafting a sigil for a pet or a child unable to express their consent—exercise thoughtful caution. Here, the litmus test is your intent: are you genuinely acting in the best interest of the subject, without any potential harm or manipulation? If so, proceed, but tread carefully, always considering the potential ramifications of your actions.

## Cultural Sensitivity and Appropriation

Sigils often draw on a wide array of symbols, many of which have roots in specific cultures or spiritual traditions. When you borrow from these sources, it's crucial to be sensitive to their origins and meanings. Understand the cultural and historical context of a symbol before incorporating it into your sigil. Improper use of sacred symbols can be seen as cultural appropriation—a form of theft that disrespects the tradition it came from.

Before using symbols from another culture or tradition, ask yourself the following questions:

- Am I educated about the deep meanings and uses of this symbol within its original culture?
- Is it appropriate for someone from outside the culture to use this symbol?
- Am I employing the symbol with respect, or am I diluting or corrupting its meaning?

## Responsible Use of Personal Power

When you craft a sigil, you channel your intention and focus into it, imbuing it with a sort of personal power. It's essential to wield this power responsibly. Avoid crafting sigils that aim to control or manipulate other individuals, as that not only violates their autonomy but also may rebound in unintended ways. For example, crafting a sigil to make someone fall in love with you doesn't just encroach on their free will—it sets up an imbalance of power in the relationship that's likely to be unhealthy for both parties involved.

## Case Study: The Ethical Pitfall of Jane's Friendship Sigil

Jane had recently grown apart from her friend Emily and decided to craft a sigil to strengthen their friendship. However, she didn't inform Emily about this. A few weeks after activating the sigil, Emily started to feel an inexplicable sense of obligation and guilt towards Jane. This led to a complicated emotional situation that eventually strained their friendship even more. If Jane had considered the ethical implications, she might have avoided the negative consequences that followed.

## Summary

Ethics in sigil crafting isn't just a philosophical afterthought; it's a critical aspect of responsible practice. Always remember the importance of consent, exercise cultural sensitivity, and be mindful of the power dynamics you're setting up. As you deepen your engagement with this transformative art, these ethical considerations serve as guiding principles that protect not just your well-being, but the well-being of those around you.

# CHAPTER 20: SYMBOLIC ARCHETYPES AND JUNGIAN PSYCHOLOGY

As you delve deeper into the transformative art of sigil crafting for self-care, it's fascinating to explore the symbiotic relationship between symbols and the psyche. A prolific body of work in this context has been contributed by Swiss psychiatrist Carl Gustav Jung. He emphasized the impact of symbolic archetypes on human behavior and consciousness. This chapter elucidates how understanding these Jungian principles can enhance your sigil crafting experience, touching upon the collective unconscious, the role of archetypes, and ways to effectively incorporate these in your sigils.

## The Collective Unconscious and Its Symbols

Jung introduced the concept of the "collective unconscious," a shared mental framework inherited by all humans. This reservoir of experiences contains universal archetypes and symbols that have been part of human history across cultures and epochs. When crafting sigils, tapping into these universally recognized symbols can amplify the efficacy of your creations. For example, using the symbol of a circle, which often represents unity or wholeness, in a sigil designed for personal harmony, may resonate deeply within the collective unconscious of not just you but also those who interact with it. Essentially, you are wielding the power of collective symbolism to accentuate your personal intention.

## Role of Archetypes in Sigil Crafting

Archetypes are essentially idealized models of personhood or concepts that resonate universally. Jung identified several such archetypes like the Hero, the Mother, the Wise Old Man, and so on. When incorporated into sigils, these can act as powerful focal points of intention and transformation.

For example, if you are crafting a sigil to enhance your personal courage, incorporating elements that resonate with the 'Hero' archetype could imbue your sigil with a layer of universal understanding and acceptance. This might include a simplified sword or shield symbol within the sigil. The idea is to harness the innate power of these archetypes that already reside in the collective unconscious to reinforce the power of your crafted symbols.

## Practical Incorporation of Jungian Concepts in Sigil Crafting

While the principles sound theoretical, their application is profoundly practical. To start, identify the primary intention behind your sigil—be it strength, love, peace, or any other concept. Next, research the various archetypes or universal symbols associated with this concept. Integrate these into your design, paying attention to balance and harmony within the sigil. Remember, less is often more; the simpler the design, the easier it is for the subconscious to process.

### Case Study: Sarah's Journey Toward Self-Love

Sarah was struggling with self-esteem issues and decided to craft a sigil aimed at bolstering self-love. She did some research and found that the 'Anima' and 'Animus,' representing the inner feminine and masculine according to Jung, could be the archetypes to focus on. Sarah designed a sigil that incorporated both the moon and the sun, symbols often associated with these archetypes. Over time, she found her relationship with herself improving, feeling a balance and completeness she hadn't felt before.

### Summary

The field of Jungian psychology offers a treasure trove of insights that can elevate your sigil crafting to an entirely new plane. By incorporating universally resonant symbols and archetypes, you don't just create a personal symbol; you create one steeped in the collective symbolism of human experience. Understanding and applying the principles of the collective unconscious and archetypes can significantly boost the potency of your sigils, making them not just personally meaningful but universally powerful.

# CHAPTER 21: EMPOWERMENT THROUGH GENDER-SPECIFIC SIGILS

Sigils offer an incredible array of applications for emotional and psychological well-being. Another layer of specificity can be added by designing sigils tailored to gender-specific needs and experiences. Gender plays a role in how societal pressures, expectations, and emotional experiences manifest in individuals. Therefore, sigils that are designed with this layer of understanding can serve as incredibly powerful tools for self-care and empowerment. This chapter explores the nuance of gender in the realm of sigil crafting, focusing on the importance of recognizing gender-specific experiences, the types of symbols that might resonate, and practical applications.

**Recognizing Gender-Specific Experiences in Emotional Well-Being**

It's crucial to acknowledge that emotional experiences and challenges can vary based on gender. For example, women often face gender-specific challenges like emotional labor, workplace discrimination, or societal pressures around beauty standards. Men, on the other hand, may grapple with toxic masculinity, emotional repression, or societal expectations to be the primary breadwinner. Non-binary or gender-nonconforming individuals face their unique set of challenges related to societal acceptance and identity validation. Crafting sigils that directly address these gender-based experiences can result in a more targeted impact, offering emotional release and empowerment that's closely aligned with the individual's lived experiences.

## Types of Symbols for Gender-Specific Sigils

When crafting gender-specific sigils, the types of symbols you choose can add another layer of resonance. For instance, feminine symbols like the moon, water, or the Venus symbol might resonate more if you're crafting a sigil focused on feminine energy or challenges. Masculine symbols like the sun, mountains, or the Mars symbol may be more appropriate for masculine-oriented goals. For non-binary or gender-nonconforming individuals, symbols that signify balance, unity, or fluidity—such as the yin-yang or infinity symbol—can be powerful.

However, it's crucial to note that these are merely starting points and not rigid guidelines. The most important factor is personal resonance; choose symbols that you connect with, irrespective of conventional gender associations.

## Practical Applications: Gender-Specific Case Studies

Alex's Sigil for Emotional Freedom

Alex identified as a man and was struggling with emotional repression due to societal expectations around masculinity. He chose symbols like a broken chain and an open heart to signify emotional freedom and vulnerability. The sigil acted as a constant reminder for Alex to break free from emotional shackles and embrace a more holistic sense of self.

Taylor's Sigil for Gender Fluidity

Taylor, who identified as gender-fluid, wanted to create a sigil to help navigate the societal challenges they faced. They chose the infinity symbol, signifying fluidity and boundlessness, and merged it with a tree, representing growth and grounding. Taylor found that focusing on this sigil during meditation helped them feel more anchored and confident in their identity.

Zara's Sigil for Empowerment in the Workplace

Zara, a woman in a male-dominated work environment, felt she needed to assert herself more. She incorporated symbols of a lioness and a crown into her sigil, representing courage and leadership. Whenever she had an important meeting or presentation, she would focus on this sigil and found that it gave her an added sense of empowerment.

## Summary

Crafting gender-specific sigils opens up a path for even more focused self-care and empowerment. By acknowledging the unique emotional experiences tied to gender, and by choosing symbols that resonate on this level, you can create powerful tools for transformation. Whether you're combating gender-specific societal expectations or seeking to affirm your identity, the incorporation of gender-sensitive symbols and intentions can significantly amplify the positive impact of your sigils.

# CHAPTER 22: CULTURAL SENSITIVITY IN SYMBOL CHOICE

Crafting sigils for self-care isn't just an individual journey; it's one that can be deeply affected by the wider culture and traditions that you are a part of, or that you interact with. Given that sigils often employ various symbols and archetypes, being culturally sensitive in your symbol choices is not just respectful—it's also essential for the efficacy of the sigil. This chapter will delve into the importance of cultural sensitivity in choosing symbols, the pitfalls of cultural appropriation, and how to ensure the symbols you select are respectful and appropriate.

## Importance of Cultural Sensitivity in Symbol Selection

Symbols are more than just drawings or designs; they often carry deeply ingrained meanings, rooted in cultural, historical, or religious contexts. For example, the Swastika is a symbol that has very different meanings in Western and Eastern cultures. While it is an ancient symbol representing prosperity and power in Hinduism, Buddhism, and Jainism, it was co-opted by the Nazis and now symbolizes hate and oppression in much of the Western world. This stark difference illustrates why understanding the cultural significance of symbols is essential when creating a sigil.

Choosing a symbol that has a culturally sensitive meaning ensures that the energy and intention you are putting into your sigil are accurately received and processed. It also minimizes the risk of unintentionally causing offense or perpetuating harmful stereotypes. Essentially, being culturally sensitive in your symbol choice makes your sigil more effective and respectful.

### The Pitfalls of Cultural Appropriation

Cultural appropriation is the adoption or use of elements from another culture, particularly when those elements are used outside their original cultural context in a way that trivializes or disrespects their importance. In the context of sigil crafting, using a sacred or significant symbol from a culture you're not a part of, without understanding its meaning and significance, is a form of cultural appropriation.

For example, incorporating Native American tribal symbols, African Adinkra symbols, or Aboriginal Australian art motifs into your sigil without an understanding and respect for their cultural significance can be problematic. These actions can perpetuate harmful stereotypes, contribute to the erasure of cultural identities, and offend individuals who belong to these cultures.

### How to Choose Symbols Responsibly

So how can you ensure that the symbols you choose for your sigils are culturally sensitive? Here are some guidelines:

- Do Your Research: Always investigate the origins and

meanings of the symbols you intend to use. Know what culture they come from, what they signify within that culture, and whether they are sacred or taboo.

- Ask for Permission: If you wish to use a symbol from a specific cultural or religious tradition, consult with someone from that culture or faith. Gain their perspective on the appropriateness of using such a symbol for your personal use.

- Context Matters: Always consider the context in which you'll be using the sigil. A symbol that is acceptable in one context may not be in another.

- Be Open to Alternatives: Sometimes the most respectful choice is to opt for a different symbol that conveys a similar meaning but doesn't carry the risk of appropriation or offense.

## Case Study: Emily's Journey in Symbol Choice

Emily wanted to create a sigil for inner peace and was initially attracted to the Om symbol, commonly used in Hinduism, Buddhism, and Jainism. However, being from a Western background with no ties to these traditions, she did some research. Emily learned about the deep spiritual significance of Om and realized that using it without full understanding could be disrespectful. Instead, she opted for a universally recognized symbol of peace, ensuring her sigil was both effective and culturally sensitive.

## Summary

Being culturally sensitive in choosing symbols for your sigils is not just an ethical necessity; it also enhances the effectiveness of the sigils by ensuring that the symbols used align well with the intended goals. Avoiding cultural appropriation by doing your research, seeking permission, and considering the context can go a long way in making your sigil crafting respectful and meaningful. By taking these steps, you contribute to a more respectful and inclusive environment, both for yourself and for others.

# CHAPTER 23: DIGITAL SIGILS FOR MODERN SELF-CARE

As we journey further into the digital age, the realms of ancient practices and modern technology often intersect in fascinating ways. Sigil crafting is no exception to this confluence. While the traditional ways of crafting sigils involved paper, ink, and other physical materials, digital platforms offer new avenues for creation and utilization. In this chapter, we will explore the emerging concept of digital sigils, the platforms and tools that can be used to create them, and the ethical considerations to keep in mind.

### The Rise of Digital Sigils

Digital sigils are graphical symbols crafted and utilized via digital platforms. From computer-generated designs to augmented reality applications, the digital world provides a broad canvas for innovation. The same principles of intention, focus, and symbolic representation apply, whether you are crafting a sigil on parchment with a quill or designing one on a digital canvas.

Digital sigils offer a set of advantages and challenges that are unique to their medium. One significant advantage is accessibility. Tools for digital design are widely available and often free, making it easier for people to try their hand at sigil crafting. These sigils can be shared effortlessly across distances, making them highly versatile. The ability to animate digital sigils introduces a dynamic element that isn't possible with static, physical designs. Animation can amplify the intention behind a sigil, as movement is another form of symbolism that can carry meaning.

However, this ease of use and shareability also brings forth ethical considerations. Since digital sigils can be easily copied and distributed, the questions of authorship and consent become even more critical. Also, the risk of your work being used in a manner contrary to its intended purpose is worth noting.

## Tools and Platforms for Crafting Digital Sigils

The avenues for creating digital sigils are as varied as the apps and software available for graphic design. Here are some commonly used platforms:

- Graphic Design Software: Programs like Adobe Illustrator or free alternatives like GIMP offer extensive features for intricate design work.

- Drawing Tablets: If you enjoy the tactile experience of drawing but want the benefits of a digital medium, drawing tablets can be an excellent choice.

- Mobile Apps: There are now apps designed specifically for sigil crafting, complete with libraries of symbols and customizable features.

- Augmented Reality: For those who are technologically savvy, AR offers a compelling medium to layer your sigils over the real world, accessible via smartphones or AR glasses.

## Case Study: Mark's Experience with Digital Sigils

Mark was an avid practitioner of sigil magic who also happened to be a software developer. Melding his interests, he developed an app that allowed users to craft sigils easily. Using machine learning algorithms, the app could also suggest symbols based on the intentions the user inputted. Mark always emphasized the importance of personalized intent, reminding users that the app was a tool to aid but not replace their personal connection to their sigils.

## Ethical Considerations in Digital Sigil Crafting

While digital platforms offer exciting possibilities, they also present a unique set of ethical challenges. Copyright issues are at the forefront, as the digital medium makes it easy to copy and disseminate work. Always respect the intellectual property of others and seek permission if you plan to use someone else's design.

Additionally, think about the consent and intentionality when sharing sigils. Remember, a sigil is a deeply personal creation imbued with specific intentions. When a sigil is shared without context or permission, its impact can be diluted or misused. Always provide context and seek consent when sharing digital sigils.

## Summary

The fusion of ancient sigil crafting with modern technology offers both exciting opportunities and ethical considerations. Digital sigils extend the accessibility, versatility, and dynamism of this time-honored practice. Yet they also demand a heightened awareness of ethics, particularly concerning authorship, copyright, and the sharing of personal intentions. As with traditional forms, the core tenets of intentionality, focus, and respect continue to be the cornerstone of digital sigil crafting.

# CHAPTER 24: THE ROLE OF ARTISTIC EXPRESSION IN SIGIL CRAFTING

The melding of artistic expression and sigil crafting offers an enriching avenue for personal transformation and well-being. Not merely a means to an end, the creative process itself can serve as a therapeutic exercise that enhances the impact of the sigils you produce. Today, we will delve into the profound link between art and sigil crafting, the diverse styles and mediums that you can explore, and how artistic self-expression serves as a potent catalyst for emotional and psychological healing.

## Art as Process and Product in Sigil Crafting

Traditionally, sigil crafting has focused on the product—the final sigil—as the agent of transformation. However, modern psychology illuminates the therapeutic value of the creative process itself. The act of drawing, painting, or even sculpting a sigil can be deeply meditative, serving as a form of mindfulness that allows you to become fully immersed in the moment. This focused attention not only reinforces your intention behind the sigil but also provides a pathway for emotional release and mental clarity.

Artistic techniques such as color blending, pattern variation, and texture exploration can deepen the layers of symbolism in a sigil. For example, using watercolors to create a fluid, blended look could symbolize the smooth integration of different emotions or states of mind. On the other hand, bold, sharp lines might represent clarity, focus, or unyielding determination. These artistic choices, far from being arbitrary aesthetic preferences, contribute to the energy and purpose of the sigil.

## Case Study: Samantha's Artistic Sigils

Samantha, a professional artist, found herself struggling with bouts of depression and anxiety. Already versed in the therapeutic aspects of her art, she decided to integrate sigil crafting into her painting sessions. Samantha began by sketching her sigils on canvas, then layering them with abstract patterns and vibrant colors that aligned with her intentions. The act of painting became a ritual, the layers of paint symbolizing the layers of her emotional complexity. Within a few months, not only did she feel more emotionally balanced, but she had also created a series of art pieces that were imbued with personal meaning and healing power.

## Diverse Styles and Mediums

The realm of artistic expression is vast, and there is no single "correct" way to integrate art into sigil crafting. Here are some suggestions for those who are looking to expand their artistic horizons:

- Collage: Incorporating various materials such as fabric, paper, or even metal into a collage can make your sigil multidimensional, both literally and symbolically.

- Digital Art: Utilizing graphic design software allows for precision and the easy incorporation of complex patterns and elements.

- Mixed Media: Combining traditional and digital art, or incorporating different artistic elements like sculpture and painting, can produce a uniquely impactful sigil.

Each medium and style offers a different set of symbolic tools. The choice of medium is, in itself, an act of self-expression that informs the effectiveness and meaning of the final product.

## Artistic Expression as a Catalyst for Healing

Art therapy has long been recognized for its effectiveness in treating a variety of psychological conditions, including anxiety, depression, and post-traumatic stress disorder. The act of externalizing your emotions through artistic creation can bring clarity and perspective. Furthermore, the tangible result—a piece of art imbued with intent—serves as a continual reminder and activator of the healing process. Thus, incorporating artistic expression into sigil crafting multiplies the avenues through which healing can occur.

## Summary

Integrating artistic expression into the process of sigil crafting adds depth, richness, and multifaceted avenues for personal transformation. The art-based approach respects both the journey —the creative process—and the destination—the completed sigil. It opens the door to a variety of artistic styles and mediums, allowing for a more personalized and enriched experience. Far more than just an aesthetic choice, your artistic engagement in crafting sigils amplifies their efficacy and turns the creative process into a catalytic agent for emotional and psychological well-being.

# CHAPTER 25: SIGILS AND SPIRITUAL WELL-BEING

The tapestry of human well-being extends beyond mere physical or psychological health; spiritual well-being is an integral part of this holistic view. The practice of crafting sigils can be a conduit for deepening your spiritual connection, anchoring metaphysical concepts in tangible form, and facilitating transformative experiences. In this chapter, we will explore the multifaceted relationship between sigils and spiritual health, delve into the ways sigils can function as spiritual tools, and examine the ethical considerations that arise in this domain.

## Sigils as Spiritual Anchors

Sigils, by their very nature, are condensed symbols that represent complex intentions or ideas. When it comes to spiritual well-being, they can serve as powerful anchors that remind us of our innate interconnectedness with the universe, spiritual values, or specific religious teachings. People often use sigils to embody spiritual tenets such as compassion, inner peace, and divine connection. These spiritual anchors can be integrated into meditation, prayer, or other ritualistic practices, enhancing focus and presence.

In many spiritual traditions, the power of symbols is well recognized. From the Christian cross to the Buddhist mandala, symbols have always been used as focal points for contemplation and communion with the divine. The act of creating a sigil with spiritual intent imbues it with a unique resonance that aligns with your personal beliefs and experiences.

## Case Study: Jonathan's Spiritual Journey

Jonathan, a lifelong seeker, struggled to maintain a consistent spiritual practice. Feeling overwhelmed by various rituals and dogmas, he turned to sigil crafting as a personalized, less dogmatic approach to spirituality. He crafted sigils for different aspects of his spiritual life, such as mindfulness, divine connection, and empathy. Over time, he noticed that these sigils became focal points during his meditation, allowing him to tap into a deeper level of spiritual awareness. These simple yet powerful symbols helped him navigate his spiritual path without the weight of rigid practices.

## The Role of Ritual and Ceremony

The creation and activation of a sigil can be enhanced through ritual or ceremony, elements often found in spiritual practices. The process of ritualization sanctifies your intentions and deepens your connection with the sigil. Ritual can be as simple as lighting a candle while drawing your sigil, or as elaborate as a full ceremony that includes chants, offerings, or the invocation of deities.

Ritual actions performed during the crafting or activation of a sigil can align your energy and focus, lending your work greater potency. Moreover, a well-designed ritual provides a structured environment that can facilitate the safe exploration of spiritual realms, serving as a buffer against potential negative experiences or energies.

## Ethical Considerations in Spiritual Sigil Crafting

When crafting sigils for spiritual well-being, it's crucial to navigate ethical considerations consciously. Spiritual well-being is a deeply personal and often sensitive area, and your sigil crafting should respect the diversity of beliefs and experiences, both your own and others'. Avoid the appropriation of symbols from religious or spiritual traditions to which you do not belong or understand, as this can be both disrespectful and potentially harmful.

Ensure that your intentions are clear, positive, and in alignment with your spiritual values. If you're using sigils in a group setting, make sure that the symbols and intentions are inclusive and respectful of all participants. The ethical crafting of spiritual sigils will contribute to a more authentic and powerful spiritual practice.

## Summary

Sigils can serve as potent tools for enhancing spiritual well-being. As symbolic anchors, they can embody complex spiritual tenets or values, offering a personalized approach to spiritual practice. The incorporation of rituals or ceremonies amplifies the potency and focus of sigil crafting, aligning it more closely with traditional spiritual practices. However, ethical considerations, particularly the respect for diverse spiritual beliefs and practices, should guide your crafting process. Whether you are a seasoned spiritual practitioner or someone seeking a flexible, personalized path, sigils offer a creative and impactful means of enhancing your spiritual life.

# CHAPTER 26:
# UTILIZING TAROT AND ORACLE CARDS FOR SIGIL INSPIRATION

The rich tapestry of symbolism and archetypes found in Tarot and Oracle cards offers a treasure trove of inspiration for sigil crafting. While sigils are highly personalized symbols created to manifest specific desires or intentions, Tarot and Oracle cards come with their own set of established meanings that have been developed over centuries. The intersection of these two symbolic systems can lead to an enriched understanding of both, enhancing the effectiveness of your sigils while imbuing them with deeper, multi-layered meanings. In this chapter, we'll delve into how you can effectively draw inspiration from these cards, the creative process of blending symbols, and the nuances of attributing meaning to your sigils.

**Drawing Inspiration from Tarot and Oracle Cards**

Tarot cards are comprised of a set of 78 cards divided into the Major Arcana and Minor Arcana, each with their own symbolic meaning. Oracle cards, on the other hand, may not have a fixed number of cards or set meanings, allowing for a more intuitive and flexible use. Both sets of cards offer a rich narrative told through symbols, numbers, colors, and archetypes. Whether you're pulling cards to gain insights into specific situations or using them for daily guidance, the imagery and symbolism can be a direct source of inspiration for your sigils.

For instance, if you're working on a sigil to enhance your creative energies, you might draw inspiration from The Empress card in the Tarot, which symbolizes fertility, creativity, and nurturing. You can borrow elements from this card—like the Venus symbol, the pomegranates, or even the twelve stars in the crown—to incorporate into your sigil.

## Case Study: Emily's Creative Block

Emily, an artist, faced a prolonged creative block. She used a Tarot spread to seek guidance and pulled The Empress, The Magician, and The Star cards. Inspired, she created a sigil that incorporated elements from all three cards: the Venus symbol from The Empress for creativity, the lemniscate from The Magician for infinite possibilities, and the water jug from The Star for hope and inspiration. This personalized sigil acted as a catalyst, helping her overcome her block and reignite her creative spark.

## Blending Symbols for Enhanced Potency

Another fascinating avenue of exploration is blending the symbols of Tarot and Oracle cards to create composite sigils. This process takes advantage of the multi-layered meanings inherent in each card, making your sigils robust, complex, and enriched. For example, combining the Wheel of Fortune and Justice cards might give you a sigil focused on fair outcomes in situations of change or uncertainty.

When blending symbols, consider the balance between the elements you choose. You can pick aspects that are complementary or contrasting, depending on your goal. The key is to be intuitive yet intentional in your selection, creating a sigil that feels both potent and true to your aims.

## Nuances of Attributing Meaning

When you're drawing inspiration from Tarot and Oracle cards, remember that you're entering a space laden with centuries of interpretation and cultural significance. Each card carries multiple meanings, both traditional and personal. As you craft your sigil, it's crucial to define what each symbol or element you're incorporating means to you.

Take, for example, the Death card. While traditionally it symbolizes the end of a cycle and the beginning of a new one, some people might have a different, personal interpretation. When using elements from this card, be clear about the particular aspect of its symbolism you are utilizing. The power of your sigil lies not just in the universal meanings but also in your personal relationship to those symbols.

## Summary

Utilizing Tarot and Oracle cards as inspiration for sigil crafting adds a new layer of depth and intricacy to your work. Drawing on the rich symbolism and narratives these cards provide allows you to craft sigils that are uniquely potent. By blending elements from different cards, you can create composite sigils with amplified meanings. However, remember that attributing your personal meanings to these symbols is crucial for effective sigil crafting. Whether you are a seasoned card reader or a beginner, the interplay between sigils and these cards offers a fertile ground for creativity and manifestation.

# CHAPTER 27: MANIFESTATION AND LAW OF ATTRACTION WITH SIGILS

The concept of manifestation and the Law of Attraction has been circulating in mainstream culture for some time. While various forms of these principles have existed in esoteric and spiritual traditions for centuries, their fusion with modern psychology and wellness practices has reinvigorated their application. In essence, both concepts revolve around the idea that one can draw experiences, opportunities, and even material objects into one's life through focused intent. Sigils, with their direct and visual nature, can serve as potent tools for manifesting these desired outcomes. This chapter will explore the synergy between sigils, manifestation, and the Law of Attraction, providing practical guidance on how to align your sigil work with these concepts for optimized results.

### Aligning Intentions: The Heart of Manifestation

At the core of any manifestation practice is the articulation and alignment of your intentions. When crafting a sigil, the intention-setting process is a crucial step, which typically involves writing a statement of intent and converting it into a symbol. However, in the context of manifestation, the intention needs to be refined and clarified further, making sure it aligns with what you genuinely desire and believe you can achieve.

For instance, if you wish to manifest better health, consider what that specifically means to you. Does it involve more energy, fewer symptoms, or perhaps a successful surgery? Your sigil's power comes from the precision and emotional resonance of your intent. This laser-focused clarity is the point where sigils and manifestation truly intersect, serving as a catalyst to draw your desired outcome into reality.

## Case Study: Thomas and Financial Stability

Thomas was struggling with financial instability and decided to engage in a manifestation practice alongside crafting sigils. He was initially tempted to set a vague intention like "I want to be wealthy." However, upon deeper reflection, he realized that his actual desire was for financial stability, not just accumulating wealth. He crafted a sigil with the precise intention: "I manifest financial stability and consistent income." Over the subsequent months, Thomas found himself making wiser financial decisions, and opportunities for stable income presented themselves.

## The Role of Emotional Resonance

Another pillar of effective manifestation is emotional resonance, or the emotional charge your intention carries. According to the Law of Attraction, like attracts like; thus, positive emotional energy would attract positive outcomes. In the realm of sigil crafting, the activation phase—where you infuse the sigil with energy—plays a critical role in determining its emotional resonance. Techniques such as meditation, breath control, or even dance can help to heighten your emotional state, ensuring that the sigil is charged with the kind of energy conducive to attraction and manifestation.

### Repetition and Reinforcement: Sigils in Daily Practice

While crafting and activating a sigil are essential steps, repetition and reinforcement can amplify their power, especially when using them for manifestation. Displaying your sigils in places where you'll frequently encounter them, or incorporating them into daily rituals or meditations, can serve as a constant reminder and reinforcement of your intentions.

This repetitive reinforcement serves a dual purpose. Firstly, it ensures that your intent stays at the forefront of your mind, subtly steering your actions and decisions in the direction of your goals. Secondly, it amplifies the emotional resonance over time, effectively "feeding" the sigil's energy, making it a more potent magnet for your manifestations.

### Summary

Manifestation and the Law of Attraction are principles that focus on drawing desired experiences and outcomes into one's life through intent and emotional resonance. When integrated with the practice of sigil crafting, these principles offer a potent method for manifesting those intentions. By aligning your sigils with precise, emotionally resonant intentions and incorporating them into a regular practice of reinforcement, you're effectively leveraging a multi-faceted approach to bring your desires into reality. Whether you're new to the concept of manifestation or a seasoned practitioner, integrating it with sigil craft offers a dynamic, enriching, and effective avenue for achieving your life goals.

# CHAPTER 28:
# CREATING SIGILS FOR
# PHYSICAL WELLNESS

Sigils are not just a modality for emotional and psychological well-being; they can also be an incredible tool for promoting physical health. How exactly can a graphical symbol, crafted from intention and symbolized in a design, contribute to physical wellness? The answer lies in the interconnectedness of mind, body, and spirit. In this chapter, we'll explore the methodologies for crafting sigils aimed at physical health, the underlying psychology that can make these sigils effective, and the incorporation of existing medical and wellness routines to bolster their potency.

## Crafting Methodologies for Physical Wellness

Creating a sigil for physical health requires a slightly different approach compared to crafting one for emotional or psychological needs. The key here is to be as specific as possible. Unlike emotional states, which can be broad and multifaceted, physical conditions often have precise medical definitions. For instance, if you're looking to create a sigil for reducing migraines, your statement of intent should be as detailed as possible, perhaps something like, "I manifest relief from frequent migraines."

## Case Study: Emily's Quest for Digestive Health

Emily suffered from chronic digestive issues. After several medical consultations and treatments, she decided to incorporate sigils into her wellness routine. She created a sigil with the specific intention: "My digestive system functions optimally." She then placed this sigil near her dining area and also saved it as a wallpaper on her phone. Over time, along with maintaining her medical treatments, she noticed a significant improvement in her digestive health.

### The Psychological Bridge to Physical Health

Sigils can influence physical wellness through the psychological framework known as the mind-body connection. Our mental state can have a profound effect on our physical well-being. Stress, for example, has been proven to exacerbate a wide array of physical conditions, from heart disease to digestive issues.

When a sigil is crafted for a specific physical outcome, merely viewing the sigil could act as a psychological prompt that focuses your mind's attention on that particular area of wellness. This concentrated focus can stimulate the body's own healing mechanisms. Moreover, in conditions where lifestyle adjustments are beneficial—like switching to a healthier diet or incorporating exercise—the focus induced by the sigil can make adopting and maintaining these adjustments more manageable.

### Integrating Sigils with Existing Wellness Routines

While sigils can be powerful tools, it's important to remember that they are not a replacement for qualified medical advice or treatments. However, they can serve as a complementary addition to existing medical or wellness routines. If you're taking medication for a condition, for instance, crafting a sigil with the intention of "My medication works effectively for my highest good" can be a supportive step. Similarly, if you're engaged in physical therapy, a sigil to enhance the benefits of the therapy can be helpful.

## Case Study: Sarah and Her Fitness Regimen

Sarah was committed to a fitness routine but often struggled with motivation. She decided to craft a sigil with the intention: "I am energized and motivated during my workouts." She placed this sigil in her gym bag and also used it as a screensaver on her phone. Over the weeks, she observed a significant increase in her energy levels and focus during workouts.

## Summary

The application of sigils for physical wellness hinges on a blend of specificity in intention, psychological prompting, and integration with existing medical or wellness practices. Crafting a sigil for a targeted physical condition, keeping in mind the depth of the mind-body connection, can yield promising results. When integrated respectfully and sensibly into existing health routines, sigils can serve as an empowering adjunct tool for enhancing your physical well-being. Whether you're dealing with chronic conditions, or simply striving for a healthier lifestyle, sigils offer a uniquely personal and focused means to support your journey to physical wellness.

# CHAPTER 29: CASE STUDIES: REAL-LIFE APPLICATIONS OF SIGILS FOR SELF-CARE

The concept of using sigils for self-care may seem esoteric or theoretical until you see them in action, impacting real lives in tangible ways. The journeys of individuals who have utilized sigils effectively provide us not only with proof of their practical utility but also offer insights into how these potent symbols can be seamlessly integrated into various aspects of daily life. In this chapter, we'll delve into three compelling case studies that showcase the versatility and effectiveness of sigils for self-care.

### Case Study 1: Laura's Triumph Over Social Anxiety

Laura had battled social anxiety for years. Traditional methods, such as medication and therapy, provided some relief but didn't quite resolve her issues. She decided to add sigil crafting into her repertoire of coping strategies. Laura focused her intention on social ease and confidence, crafting a sigil that embodied these qualities. She drew the sigil on a small piece of paper and kept it in her wallet, making it a point to touch it before entering social situations. Over time, Laura noted that her levels of anxiety reduced significantly, and she was able to engage in social activities with a newfound confidence. It was as if the sigil served as both a psychological anchor and a catalyst, triggering an internal change that was reflected in her external world.

## Case Study 2: Tim's Journey Towards Financial Stability

Tim was a freelance graphic designer who struggled with irregular income and financial instability. Though he possessed the skills needed for his job, he was plagued by procrastination and a lack of focus, which severely impacted his earnings. After learning about the power of sigils, Tim decided to craft one with the intention of "financial stability and productivity." He created a desktop wallpaper out of his sigil and set reminders on his phone to gaze at it for a few minutes every day.

Slowly but surely, Tim began to notice changes in his behavior. He found himself more focused and efficient, often completing projects ahead of schedule. This increased productivity led to more job opportunities and eventually, the financial stability he had been seeking. For Tim, the sigil acted as a focal point for his scattered energies, helping him channel them into productive endeavors.

## Case Study 3: Susan's Balancing Act with Emotional Well-Being

Susan was someone who had always struggled with mood swings and emotional imbalance. Although she tried various methods to achieve emotional equilibrium, from medication to meditation, she often felt like she was on a roller coaster. Susan came across the concept of sigils and decided to give it a shot. Her sigil's intention was "emotional balance and harmony." She drew this sigil on a small stone and kept it on her office desk as a constant reminder.

Within weeks, Susan started experiencing a more stable emotional state. It wasn't that her challenges magically disappeared; rather, she felt better equipped to handle them. Whenever she found herself spiraling into emotional turbulence, a glance at her sigil helped her regain her composure. The sigil served as a symbolic tether, grounding her when her emotions threatened to carry her away.

## Summary

Laura, Tim, and Susan come from different backgrounds and struggled with distinct issues, yet they all found solace and support through the incorporation of sigils into their self-care practices. These case studies demonstrate that the art of sigil crafting is versatile and can be tailored to suit individual needs, whether it's combating social anxiety, achieving financial stability, or maintaining emotional balance. The experiences of these individuals underscore the transformative potential of sigils, making them an invaluable addition to a comprehensive approach to self-care.

# CHAPTER 30: ASTROLOGICAL INSIGHTS FOR SIGIL CRAFTING

Astrology and sigil crafting may seem like disparate realms at first glance, but when combined, they can offer a nuanced and highly personalized approach to self-care. The idea here isn't to conflate the two, but to explore how the rich symbolism and nuanced psychological insights from astrology can complement the focused intentionality of sigils. In this chapter, we'll delve into how astrological elements, such as zodiac signs, planetary influences, and houses, can serve as rich sources of inspiration and guidance for crafting highly potent sigils.

**Zodiac Signs as Symbolic Influences**

Each zodiac sign possesses its own unique set of characteristics, and these traits can be beneficial in defining the intent behind your sigil. For example, if you are an Aries seeking courage, crafting a sigil that incorporates the fiery, bold characteristics of your zodiac sign could amplify its effectiveness. Or perhaps you're a Libra aiming for harmony in relationships; a sigil inspired by Libran traits of balance and diplomacy can be incredibly potent.

To give it more context, let's consider the case of Emily, who is a Cancer. Emily was looking for emotional stability and wanted to create a sigil to help with that. She researched the core qualities of her zodiac sign—empathy, nurturing, and emotional depth—and incorporated them into her sigil design. Over time, Emily found that this personalized sigil was particularly effective in helping her manage emotional highs and lows.

## Planetary Influences in Crafting Sigils

Astrology teaches us that each planet governs specific areas of human life. Mars, for instance, rules over action and desire, while Venus is the planet of love and beauty. You can leverage these associations when crafting a sigil. Say you want to improve your communication skills; you might design a sigil inspired by the attributes of Mercury, the planet of communication. This adds another layer of symbolism and intent to your sigil, making it more targeted and, potentially, more effective.

Let's look at another example: Robert, who wanted to advance in his career, chose to craft a sigil inspired by Saturn, the planet associated with discipline and long-term success. By doing so, Robert found that he was able to better focus on his career goals, and over time he witnessed a marked improvement in his professional life.

## Houses and Their Role in Sigil Crafting

In astrology, the natal chart is divided into twelve houses, each ruling different areas of life, from self-identity to career, relationships, and beyond. Using the symbolism of houses can also be a deeply personalized way to craft sigils. For instance, if you want to work on self-improvement, you might draw inspiration from the attributes of the First House, which is all about self and identity.

Consider the case of Sarah. Struggling with issues related to self-esteem, she decided to create a sigil inspired by the Fourth House, which governs our emotional foundation and home life. Sarah felt a profound connection to her sigil and found that it helped her gain emotional strength over time.

## Summary

Integrating astrological insights into your sigil crafting process adds another layer of personalization and depth to your symbols. Whether it's channeling the traits of your zodiac sign, harnessing the unique energies of specific planets, or drawing inspiration from the astrological houses, these astrological elements can lend your sigils additional potency and specificity. Through the fusion of these ancient systems—astrology and sigil craft—you can create symbols that are not only visually striking but also deeply resonant with your unique psychological makeup and life circumstances.

# CHAPTER 31:
# CRAFTING SIGILS
# FOR RELATIONSHIP
# HEALING

Relationships are complex tapestries woven from threads of emotion, psychology, and shared experiences. When strains or knots form in this intricate weave, they can profoundly affect our emotional well-being. Crafting sigils specifically aimed at relationship healing can serve as a powerful adjunct to more traditional forms of relational therapy or dialogue. Let's delve into how you can craft sigils to enhance communication, rebuild trust, and foster emotional bonds in your relationships.

## Sigils for Enhanced Communication

Communication is the cornerstone of any successful relationship. A breakdown in communication can lead to misunderstandings, hurt feelings, and even the decay of the relationship itself. Crafting sigils with the specific intent of improving communication can be incredibly beneficial. To do this, you might focus on symbols that resonate with clarity, openness, and mutual understanding.

For instance, consider the case of Samantha, who had been experiencing recurring communication issues with her partner. They seemed to talk past each other, leading to frequent arguments. Samantha decided to craft a sigil focusing on the throat chakra, traditionally associated with communication, as well as symbols that represented listening and speaking. She used this sigil as a touchstone during conversations with her partner, and over time, she noticed a palpable improvement in their communication dynamics.

## Restoring Trust with Sigils

Trust is another crucial element in relationships that can be supported through sigil crafting. If you've experienced a betrayal or even just a series of misunderstandings that have eroded trust, a sigil can serve as a focal point for your intention to rebuild. Symbols that invoke feelings of safety, fidelity, and reliability can be particularly effective in these sigils.

Take the example of Alex, who had undergone a challenging period in his friendship with his long-time friend Mark due to some financial disagreements. To rebuild trust, Alex crafted a sigil incorporating symbols of balance scales, handshakes, and an unbroken circle. Alex carried this sigil with him, especially when meeting Mark, as a physical manifestation of his intent to restore equilibrium in their relationship. Over time, the atmosphere between them began to heal, and the trust was gradually re-established.

## Emotional Reconnection through Sigils

Often, relationships suffer not from any specific grievance but from a general sense of emotional distance. In such situations, sigils designed to foster emotional closeness can be invaluable. Symbols associated with the heart, interconnectedness, and emotional warmth can form the basis of such sigils.

As an example, Jennifer was feeling increasingly disconnected from her family members, especially her teenage children. To address this, she crafted a sigil that incorporated symbols like intertwined roots and a heart, symbolizing emotional connectedness and love. She placed this sigil in a communal area of the home where everyone could see it. Over weeks, Jennifer noticed subtle but definite shifts in the family dynamics, with increased emotional closeness and more meaningful interactions among all family members.

## Summary

Relationships are essential for our mental and emotional well-being, and the act of crafting sigils can serve as a meaningful ritual to mend the fractures that often appear in these intricate bonds. By focusing on specific areas such as communication, trust, and emotional connection, you can create sigils that serve as potent tools for relationship healing. They can act as focal points for your intentions, helping you navigate the complexities of human interactions with greater empathy, awareness, and hope for a harmonious future.

# CHAPTER 32: THE LINK BETWEEN MUSIC AND SIGILS

Music and symbols have one critical thing in common: they're both languages that speak to our subconscious. Music elicits emotions and memories, alters our mood, and can even impact our physical body. Similarly, sigils serve as condensed symbols filled with intent, also targeting our subconscious to trigger change. This chapter explores the fascinating synergy between music and sigils, examining how these two forms of expression can be combined for heightened self-care and psychological well-being.

**Harmonizing Sigils with Musical Elements**

To integrate music and sigils, we need to understand the building blocks of music that can pair well with the symbolic representations in sigils. The musical elements that are particularly useful in this endeavor include melody, rhythm, and frequency.

- Melody: The contour and sequence of notes can carry emotional weight. Aligning a specific melody with a sigil designed for a particular emotional intent can be powerful. For example, consider the instance of Julia, who was looking for a way to combat her chronic anxiety. She designed a sigil aimed at peace and relaxation and found a melody that also evoked these emotions. She played this melody while meditating on her sigil, which she found to be remarkably effective at calming her mind.

- Rhythm: Rhythm holds the power to evoke physical reactions. A fast rhythm can raise your heart rate, while a slow one can induce calm. Like Julia, Thomas also wanted to use a sigil for relaxation, but he found that focusing on rhythm worked better for him. He paired his sigil with a slow, steady drumbeat, and this combination helped him find a deep sense of tranquility.

- Frequency: Sound frequencies have different effects on the mind and body. High-frequency sounds are generally uplifting, while low-frequency sounds can be grounding or calming. Elaine wanted to increase her focus and concentration. She paired a sigil designed for this purpose with a piece of music that primarily used high frequencies. The result was a heightened sense of focus and attentiveness.

## Sigil Activation through Musical Rituals

Activating a sigil typically requires a form of focused energy. Music can serve as this catalyzing energy. You can incorporate musical elements into rituals that you perform to activate your sigils. Here's how:

- Create Your Sigil: Design a sigil for your specific intent.
- Choose Your Music: Find or compose music that resonates with your intent.
- Meditation and Focus: Meditate while focusing on your sigil and listening to the selected music.
- Activation: At the climax of the music, visualize your sigil glowing with energy, symbolizing its activation.

For instance, Amelia was having trouble sleeping. She created a sigil aimed at fostering peaceful sleep and chose a lullaby that she found relaxing. She would focus on the sigil while the lullaby reached its melodic peak, at which point she visualized the sigil activating. Over time, Amelia found that this ritual helped her fall asleep more quickly and improved the quality of her sleep.

## The Psychological Underpinning of Music and Sigils

Both music and sigils impact the brain's limbic system, a region associated with emotions, memories, and arousal. This suggests that the combination could create a synergistic effect, enhancing the efficacy of either when used alone. For example, consider Neil, a musician who decided to blend his love for music with sigil craft. He was working on improving his self-esteem and crafted a sigil to help with this. Neil also composed a piece of uplifting music. Every time he listened to this music, he would also meditate on his sigil. Over weeks, Neil reported a significant boost in his self-esteem levels, attributing it to this combined approach.

## Summary

Music and sigils share the unique ability to communicate directly with our subconscious. Combining these two powerful tools can create a self-care regimen that addresses both emotional and psychological needs effectively. By understanding the elements of music that pair well with the intent of your sigils, and by incorporating musical rituals for activation, you can create a harmonized system for holistic well-being. This blended approach not only adds another layer of depth to your self-care practices but also opens up new dimensions of psychological resilience and emotional balance.

# CHAPTER 33:
# CRAFTING SIGILS
# FOR WORKPLACE
# WELL-BEING

Workplace stress is a burgeoning issue affecting millions. The pressure to perform, meet deadlines, and maintain a work-life balance can take a toll on your psychological well-being. Given the amount of time we spend at work, it's critical to ensure that this environment fosters not just productivity but also emotional health. This chapter offers a tailored look at how crafting personalized sigils can be an effective tool in promoting well-being in the workplace.

**Individualized Sigils for Professional Goals**

Career-related goals often require sustained focus and effort. Traditional methods like vision boards or affirmations are widely used for motivation, but sigils can offer a more private and personalized approach. Let's examine a couple of cases:

- Motivation and Focus: Emily, a software developer, found her work becoming monotonous, affecting her motivation. She crafted a sigil with the intent of

"Focused Motivation" and placed it near her workstation. Over time, she began to notice a more keen sense of focus and a renewed interest in her tasks.

- Conflict Resolution: Mark, a manager in a logistic company, had been facing constant tension within his team. He decided to create a sigil with the intent of "Harmonious Relationships." He kept this sigil in his pocket during team meetings. Not only did the sigil act as a tangible focal point for his intention, but he also felt it subtly shifted the team dynamics over time.

By personalizing the intent behind the sigil, you can tailor it to meet specific professional challenges you might face, be they lack of motivation, tension in relationships, or even ethical quandaries.

## Creating a Positive Workspace Through Sigils

Physical environment plays a crucial role in our overall well-being. However, workplaces are often designed for efficiency rather than comfort or positivity. Yet, the ambiance can significantly influence productivity and mental health. Sigils can be an innovative approach to enhancing workspace ambiance.

- Placement Matters: Strategically placing sigils around the workspace can foster a more positive environment. You might place a sigil designed for creativity on your desk, or one for stress relief in a common area. Angela, who works in a high-stress sales environment, placed a sigil with the intent of "Calm and Balance" in the break room. She found that her colleagues appreciated it, and the overall stress levels in the office seemed to reduce.

- Desk and Gadgets: Sigils can also be incorporated into work essentials, like notebooks or gadgets. Robert, an architect, engraved a sigil aimed at "Innovative Thinking" onto the cover of his sketchbook. The symbolic reminder not only helped him mentally but seemed to spark his creativity more frequently.

## Addressing Remote Work Challenges with Sigils

The surge in remote work has brought forth unique challenges, including feelings of isolation and the blurring of work-life boundaries. Sigils can be particularly helpful in such circumstances.

- Setting Boundaries: Carrie, a freelance writer, struggled with defining work hours while working from home. She designed a sigil with the intent of "Defined Boundaries" and placed it at her home office entrance. This visual cue helped her maintain a healthier work-life balance.

- Overcoming Isolation: William, a remote customer service agent, felt isolated working alone from home. He created a sigil aimed at "Social Connectivity" and placed it near his computer. Even though he couldn't quantify the change, he felt a greater sense of connection with his team during virtual meetings.

## Summary

Workplaces are not just venues for productivity but also crucial spheres affecting our emotional and psychological health. Crafting sigils can offer a personalized approach to address common workplace challenges, from individual professional goals to cultivating a more positive workspace, and even tackling the nuances of remote work. By placing these sigils strategically, integrating them into work essentials, or using them as focal points during virtual interactions, you can foster a more balanced, harmonious, and fulfilling work environment.

# CHAPTER 34:
# THE FUTURE OF
# PSYCHOLOGICAL
# SIGIL CRAFT

As we move deeper into an era defined by unprecedented access to both traditional wisdom and modern science, the role of practices like sigil craft within the domain of mental health and emotional well-being continues to evolve. A confluence of technology, research, and cultural shifts is shaping the future of sigil craft as a viable, effective tool for psychological self-care. This chapter aims to explore emerging trends and future possibilities in psychological sigil craft, to provide you with a dynamic perspective on this ancient yet ever-relevant practice.

**Integrating Sigils with Emerging Technologies**

Digital landscapes are transforming rapidly, influencing how we interact with various forms of knowledge, including esoteric practices like sigil craft. Consider the burgeoning field of augmented reality (AR). Envision an application that allows you to see digitally superimposed sigils over your real-world environment through your smartphone. A digital sigil could hover over your workspace or even on household items that you interact with daily, serving as constant reminders or activators of the intentions they represent.

Similarly, advancements in biometric technology may soon enable personalized sigil crafting based on real-time emotional or physiological data. Imagine a wearable device that senses a spike in your stress hormones and prompts your smartphone to display a stress-reducing sigil. This would represent a fascinating blend of ancient symbolic practice with cutting-edge science, making the art of sigil craft more responsive and adaptive than ever before.

## Transdisciplinary Research and Applications

Historically, the realms of spirituality, psychology, and alternative therapies have often existed in parallel, rarely intersecting in significant ways. However, we're seeing a shift towards a more integrated, holistic model of human well-being, where multi-disciplinary research can provide novel insights.

For instance, it might be possible in the future to design controlled scientific studies that seek to measure the efficacy of sigils in conjunction with established therapies. Imagine a study comparing cognitive-behavioral therapy (CBT) alone versus CBT combined with personalized sigil crafting for treating anxiety disorders. Such studies could provide empirical evidence for the effectiveness of sigils, enabling healthcare providers to integrate this practice into mainstream therapeutic methodologies.

We might also see the development of specialized software platforms that incorporate sigil crafting into a broader ecosystem of mental health tools. These platforms could offer features like guided meditations centered around your personal sigils, or even virtual group therapy sessions focusing on sigil-related activities and discussions.

## Expanding Cultural Horizons and Ethical Implications

As the popularity of sigil craft grows, so does the need for ethical guidelines and cultural sensitivity. The globalization of information has exposed various traditions and practices to a worldwide audience. As people from diverse backgrounds engage in sigil craft, understanding and respecting the origins and nuances of different symbols become paramount.

Ethical considerations extend to the commercial realm as well. We may soon witness the rise of commercial platforms offering 'ready-made' sigils aimed at solving specific issues. While this can make the practice more accessible, it could risk diluting the intensely personal and introspective process that defines sigil crafting. Regulatory bodies might need to step in to ensure that such commercial avenues maintain the integrity and efficacy of this ancient practice.

## Summary

The future of psychological sigil craft holds an array of exciting possibilities. From integration with emerging technologies like augmented reality and biometrics to potential collaborations between disciplines like psychology, spirituality, and alternative therapies, sigil craft stands on the threshold of a new era. While the journey ahead is promising, it is fraught with ethical and cultural considerations that will require careful navigation. Ultimately, the convergence of ancient wisdom and modern innovation holds the promise of transforming this esoteric art into a widely recognized tool for self-improvement and emotional well-being.

# CHAPTER 35: COMBINING SIGILS WITH AROMATHERAPY AND ESSENTIAL OILS

When we think of self-care and emotional well-being, often our minds travel to a blend of different practices, ranging from modern medicine to ancient holistic approaches. Among these, aromatherapy and essential oils have gained immense popularity in recent years as effective methods for mood enhancement, stress reduction, and overall well-being. What if we took it a step further and combined the art of aromatherapy with the science of psychological sigil craft? This chapter dives into this compelling synergy, exploring how the amalgamation of aromatic essences and symbolic sigils can offer a multi-layered approach to self-care.

### The Power of Scents: Olfactory Impact on Emotions

The sense of smell is intricately linked to our emotional state. When you inhale an aroma, the olfactory receptors in your nose send signals to your brain, particularly to the limbic system, which governs emotions, memories, and arousal. For example, the scent of lavender is widely regarded as a natural sedative that can calm nerves, while citrus scents like lemon and orange are invigorating and can boost mood.

Now imagine integrating this olfactory experience with sigil crafting. Let's consider a hypothetical case study. Sarah, a graphic designer, often feels anxious due to her high-pressure job. She combines the calming aroma of lavender oil with a sigil designed for stress relief. She draws the sigil on a small piece of cloth and adds a few drops of the essential oil before placing it near her workspace. The scent acts as a constant activator of the sigil's intention, creating an environment conducive to relaxation and focus.

## Crafting Synergistic Rituals

One of the fascinating aspects of combining aromatherapy with sigil craft is the potential for creating unique rituals that engage multiple senses. For example, you could carve a sigil into a candle and then add essential oils that align with the intention behind the symbol. As the candle burns, not only is the form of the sigil activated, but the room also fills with a scent that resonates with that intention.

Let's dive into another example: Jason, a college student, wants to improve his concentration during study sessions. He crafts a sigil with this intention in mind and carves it into a beeswax candle. He then infuses the candle with a few drops of rosemary essential oil, known for its potential benefits in improving focus. As he lights the candle while studying, he finds himself more engrossed in his work, experiencing a synergistic effect from both the sigil and the aroma.

## Considerations and Precautions

While combining sigils with aromatherapy holds exciting potential, it's crucial to consider safety and suitability. Some essential oils may cause allergic reactions or skin irritations. Always conduct a patch test and use a carrier oil if you intend to apply any essential oil directly to the skin. Pregnant women and people with certain medical conditions should consult healthcare professionals before using essential oils. Additionally, ensure that the materials you use for crafting—such as inks or candles—are compatible with the oils and are non-toxic.

## Summary

Merging the captivating world of aromatherapy with the transformative power of psychological sigil craft opens a doorway to a richer, more holistic approach to emotional and psychological well-being. By integrating scent with symbolic intention, you create an experience that activates multiple neural pathways, amplifying the impact of each practice. While this exploration is still burgeoning, it holds the promise of delivering a multi-sensory palette for your self-care toolbox. As with any practice that involves substances like essential oils, taking appropriate precautions is vital for a safe and enriching experience.

# CHAPTER 36: SIGILS AND CRYSTAL HEALING

Crystals have long been celebrated for their metaphysical properties, often considered as conduits for healing energies. When coupled with the transformative nature of psychological sigils, a new realm of therapeutic possibilities arises. The intricate relationship between crystals and sigils offers an integrated form of self-care that can affect multiple aspects of your well-being, both emotional and physical. In this chapter, we'll delve into the fascinating integration of sigils and crystal healing, exploring the how-to's, benefits, and considerations in combining these two powerful modalities.

## Harmonizing Intentions: Matching Sigils with Crystals

Each crystal has its own unique vibrational frequency, and similar to sigils, is often associated with specific intentions or purposes. For instance, amethyst is widely used for its calming properties, while citrine is known for attracting prosperity and positive energy. When pairing a crystal with a sigil, it's crucial to align their energies based on what you hope to accomplish.

Take for example, Lisa, a yoga instructor who struggles with bouts of anxiety. She crafts a sigil aimed at peace and tranquility. To augment the power of her sigil, Lisa chooses to use an amethyst crystal, known for its calming influence. She draws the sigil on a piece of paper and places it under the crystal on her meditation altar. Each time she passes by or engages in meditation, she focuses on the sigil and the amethyst, effectively charging both with her intent.

## Techniques for Infusing Crystals with Sigils

There are various methods you can use to combine the energies of crystals and sigils, and the choice often depends on personal preferences as well as the resources available. Here are a few common techniques:

- Direct Carving: Some people choose to carve the sigil directly onto the surface of the crystal. This is most effective with softer stones like soapstone or selenite.
- Paper Under Crystal: As in Lisa's example, you can draw or write your sigil on a piece of paper and then place a crystal over it.
- Crystal Grids: For a more complex interplay of energies, you might opt for a crystal grid that incorporates your sigil at the center. Multiple crystals can be laid out in geometric patterns that emanate from the sigil, creating an energy web of sorts.

Consider Mark, a writer suffering from creative blocks. He decides to pair a sigil designed for creative flow with a piece of aventurine, a crystal believed to enhance creativity. Mark carves the sigil into the aventurine and places it on his writing desk. Whenever he sits down to write, the infused energy of the aventurine and the sigil serve to unclog his mental barriers, allowing his creative juices to flow freely.

## Safety and Ethical Considerations

Just as you would exercise caution when dealing with essential oils or other substances, there are safety measures to consider when working with crystals. Always cleanse your crystals before use to remove any lingering energies. Furthermore, be aware of the sourcing of your crystals; opt for those that are ethically mined and sold.

## Summary

Combining the energies of sigils and crystals offers a compelling, multidimensional approach to self-care and healing. By harmonizing the intentions of each modality, you amplify their individual effects, creating a synergistic blend that resonates on multiple frequencies of your well-being. From simple techniques like placing a crystal over a paper sigil to more involved methods like crystal grids, there are numerous ways to integrate these two practices. As with any form of self-care, however, it's vital to pay attention to safety guidelines and ethical considerations. Thus equipped, you stand at the threshold of a vibrant, interactive, and deeply personalized avenue for emotional and psychological well-being.

# CHAPTER 37: THE PLACE OF SIGILS IN GROUP THERAPY

Sigils, by their very nature, are usually seen as a highly individualized form of emotional and psychological healing. However, the scope of their efficacy isn't just confined to personal well-being; it can extend into communal settings, including group therapy. Utilizing sigils in a group context offers a rich tapestry of benefits and challenges, blending the collective energy of the group with the individual intent of each participant. This chapter explores how sigils can be woven into group therapy, providing fresh perspectives on collective healing through the unique lens of sigil magic.

## The Dynamics of Group Energy

The saying "the whole is greater than the sum of its parts" is especially true in the context of group therapy. Here, the communal environment can amplify individual contributions, creating a collective energy that benefits each participant. Sigils can serve as focal points around which this collective energy can coalesce. For example, all participants could focus their intent on a sigil that represents a shared therapeutic goal, such as reducing anxiety or building self-esteem.

Consider a real-world case involving "Tara's Haven," a group therapy setting for individuals recovering from substance abuse. The therapist, Dr. Nora, introduces the concept of sigil creation to help members of the group navigate through cravings. Each participant creates a personal sigil focused on strength and resilience but also engages with a collective sigil that represents the group's shared journey towards recovery. Dr. Nora finds that this approach not only adds another layer of support for each individual but also strengthens the sense of community within the group.

## Implementing Sigils in Group Sessions: Practical Steps

Integrating sigils into a group therapy setting requires careful planning to ensure that the practice enriches the therapeutic experience for all involved. Here are some practical steps therapists and group leaders can consider:

- Establish a Safe Space: Before introducing sigils, ensure that the group setting is welcoming and emotionally safe for all participants.

- Introduction and Education: Devote some time to explain what sigils are and how they can be effectively utilized in the context of group therapy.

- Collective Creation: Invite participants to engage in creating a group sigil, focused on a common objective or theme relevant to the therapy.

- Individual Exploration: Allow time for each member to share their personal sigil and the intent behind it, fostering a deeper understanding and connection within the group.

- Ongoing Engagement: Keep the group sigil visible during sessions and refer to it whenever appropriate to focus collective energy and reinforce the group's shared goals.

## Ethical and Emotional Considerations

While incorporating sigils can enrich group therapy, it also comes with ethical responsibilities. It's crucial to remember that not everyone may be open to the idea of using sigils or might have varying belief systems that do not align with this practice. Hence, participation should always be voluntary. Additionally, the therapist must be mindful of the emotional impact that such a practice could have. For instance, the process of creating a sigil might evoke strong emotional reactions that need to be sensitively managed within the group context.

## Summary

Integrating sigils into group therapy opens up new avenues for both individual and collective healing. By focusing on shared goals and intentions, the group can harness its collective energy to amplify the effects of each member's personal growth journey. However, the introduction of this practice must be approached with sensitivity, ensuring that the setting is emotionally safe and ethically sound for everyone involved. From enhancing the sense of community to providing an additional layer of symbolic support, sigils offer an innovative and enriching element to the landscape of group therapy.

# CHAPTER 38: TECHNOLOGY AND SIGILS: APPS AND SOFTWARE FOR CRAFTING

In today's digital landscape, the melding of ancient practices and modern technology isn't just feasible; it's increasingly common. With our smartphones always at hand and an array of software available for virtually any purpose, it's no surprise that sigil crafting has entered the digital realm as well. This chapter dives into how technology can augment the practice of creating and using sigils for self-care. We'll explore apps designed for sigil crafting, delve into the benefits of using software to generate symbols, and address considerations to keep in mind when blending the archaic with the cutting-edge.

## Sigil Crafting Apps: Convenience at Your Fingertips

With the ubiquity of smartphones and the increasing proliferation of apps for well-being, it was only a matter of time before sigil crafting joined the roster. Apps like "MystiGlyph" and "SymbioCraft" have sprung up to fill this niche. These platforms offer a multitude of features that can enhance your sigil practice. For instance, "MystiGlyph" provides a library of predefined symbols, colors, and shapes, allowing users to mix and match elements into a cohesive whole. Similarly, "SymbioCraft" incorporates machine learning to suggest symbols based on user input.

Take the case of Alice, a 34-year-old who has been interested in sigils but always found it overwhelming to start. She stumbled upon "MystiGlyph" and found that it simplified the process, offering her a gateway into the world of sigil crafting. The app also provided her with an unobtrusive reminder to focus on her sigil during the day, adding another layer to her practice.

### Software for the Detail-Oriented: Precision and Complexity

For those looking to take their sigil crafting to a higher level of complexity, software specifically designed for graphic design or vector drawing can offer a powerhouse of options. Programs like Adobe Illustrator or CorelDRAW provide an extensive suite of tools that can help you create intricately detailed and perfectly symmetrical sigils. The fine-tuned control offered by these platforms can bring a level of precision to your designs that is harder to achieve through hand-drawing.

Nina, a graphic designer by trade, started using CorelDRAW to create her sigils. The software's capabilities allowed her to experiment with intricate layers, blending modes, and texturing. She found that the depth and complexity she could achieve were unparalleled, and they resonated deeply with her personal aesthetic and intent.

### Digital Ethics and Environmental Impact

As with any technological application, ethical considerations should not be overlooked when using apps and software for sigil crafting. It's essential to research the app developers to ensure that they uphold privacy policies and ethical guidelines that resonate with your values. Additionally, consider the environmental impact of the technology you're using. Even seemingly inconsequential actions like downloading an app or running a software program have a carbon footprint. Making informed choices can add an additional layer of intentionality to your sigil crafting practice.

## Summary

Embracing technology in the realm of sigil crafting offers a gamut of possibilities—from the convenience of mobile apps to the intricate capabilities of professional graphic design software. These digital tools can not only make the process more accessible but also allow for a higher level of complexity in your designs. However, this fusion of the ancient and the modern comes with its own set of responsibilities. Ethical considerations and environmental impacts are essential facets to keep in mind as you navigate the digital avenues of sigil creation. All in all, technology can serve as a powerful ally in your journey toward emotional and psychological well-being through the art of crafting sigils.

# CHAPTER 39: RITUALS AND DAILY PRACTICES WITH SIGILS

The blending of symbols, psychology, and emotion is central to the art and science of crafting sigils. However, once you've created these unique forms, how can they be integrated into a daily routine or into rituals that offer greater meaning and efficacy? This chapter offers a deep dive into this subject, illuminating various ways to create rituals or daily practices that incorporate your sigils. We will discuss the concept of sacred space in ritual creation, explore how sigils can be layered into existing routines, and delve into the importance of intentionality in these practices.

## Sacred Space and Ritual Creation

Rituals often involve designated spaces, referred to as 'sacred spaces,' to enhance focus, presence, and energetic quality. In a world full of constant distractions, dedicating a particular space for your ritual work can serve as an invaluable asset. You don't necessarily need an elaborate setup; a corner of a room, a table, or even a small box where you keep your sigil crafting materials can serve the purpose.

In this space, placing your crafted sigils alongside other meaningful items—perhaps candles, crystals, or photos of loved ones—can deepen your emotional connection to the ritual. Such a setting not only adds an aesthetic appeal but also multiplies the psychological impacts of the symbols. Take Thomas, for example. He used a small table in his bedroom to set up his sacred space. This table included his hand-crafted sigils, a crystal that was gifted to him by a friend, and a small indoor plant. Every morning, Thomas would spend a few minutes focusing on the sigils while taking deep breaths. This simple act was transformative for him, reinforcing positive emotional patterns over time.

## Layering Sigils into Daily Routines

It's not always feasible to create an elaborate ritual around every sigil. Sometimes, practicality dictates a simpler approach, and that's okay. Sigils can be layered into your existing daily routines in an almost seamless fashion. This could be as straightforward as glancing at a sigil for reducing anxiety that you've set as your phone wallpaper during work breaks, or incorporating it into your nightly skincare regimen by tracing the symbol onto the bathroom mirror.

Incorporating a sigil practice into daily life could mean attaching a sigil for focus and concentration to your workstation. You might meditate on it before starting work, or simply let it be, allowing its subtle energy to permeate your workspace. Sarah, a teacher, used a sigil for patience and kindness and incorporated it into her daily planning routine. She placed the sigil next to her lesson plans and touched it before starting each class, offering her a momentary sense of peace and focus, benefiting not only her but also her students.

## Intentionality in Ritual and Routine

The most significant part of incorporating sigils into your rituals or daily practices is intentionality. Just as the crafting of the sigil required a focus on your intent, so too does its use. Whether it's a morning meditation ritual with your sigils or a brief interaction with them during a busy day, your attention and intention give these symbols their power. Even if you only have a few moments to engage with your sigils, ensuring those moments are full of concentrated intent can make all the difference.

## Summary

Rituals and daily practices with sigils provide an avenue for deepening the impact these crafted symbols can have on your emotional and psychological well-being. Whether through the creation of a sacred space designed for focused ritual work, or the more pragmatic layering of sigils into existing daily routines, the essential ingredient is your focused intent. Crafting a ritual or routine might initially require a bit of experimentation, but once a rhythm is established, these practices can serve as invaluable tools for self-improvement and emotional balance. As you make these rituals and routines your own, you extend an invitation for greater depth, nuance, and effectiveness in your sigil practice.

# CHAPTER 40: CONCLUSION: THE JOURNEY AHEAD IN SIGIL-ENHANCED SELF-CARE

As we draw this extensive exploration to a close, it's an opportune time to consider the broader picture that has emerged about the intersection of sigils, psychology, and emotional wellness. This practice of sigil crafting is not merely an esoteric endeavor; it is a confluence of art, mental health science, spiritual philosophy, and everyday practicality. Here, we'll discuss the long-term prospects of incorporating sigils into your self-care routine, the potential for community and collective growth, and a few thoughtful considerations for those who wish to delve deeper into this fascinating subject.

**The Personal Journey: Maintaining and Growing Your Sigil Practice**

As with any form of self-improvement or therapeutic intervention, consistency and evolution are key. It's not just about crafting a sigil; it's about integrating it into your life in a way that is organic and responsive to your changing needs and circumstances. The power of a sigil doesn't wane; it morphs, requiring you to revisit, reevaluate, and possibly recreate it.

One approach could involve periodic check-ins with yourself, to analyze the efficacy of your sigils. For example, if a sigil was created to alleviate anxiety, assess its impact over a month or two. Have your anxiety levels reduced? Do you find yourself calmer in situations that used to trigger you? An honest assessment will not only validate the effectiveness of your sigils but also provide insights into how they might be improved or modified.

## The Collective Horizon: Sigils in Community and Cultural Contexts

Sigils are deeply personal tools, but their transformative power isn't limited to individual use. There's vast potential for them to be employed in group settings—be it within families, among friends, or as a part of broader community healing initiatives. Imagine a group of individuals crafting sigils with a shared intent, such as communal prosperity, emotional support, or social justice. The combined focus and energy can serve as an amplifying force, rendering the symbolic action even more potent.

Take the case of a local community organization that wanted to combat rising levels of stress and anxiety among its members. They held a workshop where attendees collectively crafted a sigil for community well-being. This shared symbol was then displayed at community centers and even incorporated into the organization's newsletters. The collective act of focusing on a shared goal was not only empowering but also acted as a reminder of community support.

## Going Deeper: Further Studies and Exploration

While this book has aimed to be comprehensive, the field of sigil crafting in the context of psychological and emotional health is ever-evolving. New research is being conducted, and innovative methods are being developed that could provide even deeper insights into how sigils work at a psychological level. For those inclined, diving into related academic journals, attending workshops, or even participating in online forums can provide avenues for further growth and understanding.

## Summary

The journey into the world of sigils is much like embarking on a path of self-discovery. It offers not only a plethora of tools for individual growth but also introduces the exciting prospect of collective betterment. As you move forward, remember that the most potent sigil is the one that resonates with you, molded by your intent and cradled in your consistent focus. Whether you choose to deepen your study, adapt your practice to your evolving needs, or bring sigils into your community, the journey promises to be transformative. The path ahead in sigil-enhanced self-care is a landscape brimming with potential, beckoning those willing to explore it.

# THE END

Printed in Great Britain
by Amazon

46438135R00086